C000292785

THE
CHELSEA
FC
MISCELLANY

RICK GLANVILL

Dedicated to my wonderful mother, Bobbie Glanvill.

*'Chelsea is the smallest borough in London, but it
is certainly as variegated as the richest Russian cake.'*
John Betjeman, 1938

First published in 2012 by

The History Press
The Mill, Brimscombe Port
Stroud, Gloucestershire, GL5 2QG
www.thehistorypress.co.uk

© Rick Glanvill, 2012

The right of Rick Glanvill to be identified as the Author
of this work has been asserted in accordance with the
Copyrights, Designs and Patents Act 1988.

British Library Cataloguing in Publication Data.
A catalogue record for this book is available from the British Library.

ISBN 978 0 7524 8769 4

Typesetting and origination by The History Press
Printed in Great Britain

INTRODUCTION

I have been a supporter of Chelsea Football Club since a toddler in the early 1960s, and have written for and about the club since 1993. Throughout my experience following Chelsea has been a delight but a conundrum: the club rarely allows its supporters to be happy for a whole week uninterrupted. The trophies and triumphs are one thing, the unique roots and culture quite another. It's my belief they are equally important and I hope this is reflected in the multifarious collection of the obscure and the familiar.

Rick Glanvill, 2012

DATE OF BIRTH

On 11 March 1905, *The Times* carried the following announcement released through the Press Association under the headline 'New Professional Football Club':

> It has been decided to form a professional football club, called the Chelsea Football Club, for Stamford-bridge. Application will be made for admission to the first division of the Southern League.

As a result we can say that the club was born on 10 March 1905, a Friday. The meeting took place in an upstairs room at the Rising Sun public house, opposite the Stamford Bridge stadium. A month later the Articles of Association were drawn up by solicitor John Maltby and the lease of Stamford Bridge signed over to the club.

IMMORTAL PREDICTION

'In building up a team Chelsea have gone far afield, but whether the men will shake down together satisfactorily can at present only be surmised.'

The *Guardian*, 27 August 1905

MY WORD!

'Now, the first sign of Chelsea on the attack with Di Matteo . . . oh, and a good run upfront by Mark Hughes . . . and Di Matteo shoots – oohhh! What about this! It's possibly the quickest ever goal in a Wembley cup final! It's Roberto Di Matteo inside 45 seconds!'

BBC TV commentator John Motson reports
Roberto Di Matteo's 43-second strike in the 1997 FA Cup final

PLAYER OF THE DECADE: THE 1900s

George Hilsdon 1/9/1906 – 18/4/1912

London's East End has contributed many stars to the Chelsea constellation over the years, but the earliest was 'Gatling Gun' George – so-called because of the power and rapidity of his shooting. Discovered while Chelsea's player-manager Jackie Robertson was scouting a West Ham match for a different player, he was signed swiftly enough to join the Pensioners on tour in May 1906 – netting a hatful against opponents on the Continent. Such form spilled over into his debut and he netted 5 goals in a 9–2 galumphing over Glossop. It would be the first of three successive seasons of 25 or more goals, and on Boxing Day 1910 George became the first Pensioner to reach a century of goals. The bright lights of the West End would prove his undoing, sadly, and having represented England his star faded – in 1912 he was traded back to West Ham. Such had been his exploits a campaign was started to raise a statue in his honour. Instead he was commemorated with a weather-vane in his image, a replica of which still bodyswerves gusts of wind above the East Stand at Stamford Bridge.

164 appearances, 109 goals.

PREMIER LEAGUE – THE FIRST 20 YEARS

Chelsea were one of just seven founding members of the Premier League in 1992/93 to remain ever-present over the first 20 seasons, and one of the most successful.

Total points over 20 seasons

Manchester United	1,663
Arsenal	1,449
Chelsea	**1,402**
Liverpool	1,334
Aston Villa	1,089
Tottenham	1,086
Everton	1,034
Newcastle	1,017
Blackburn	969
Manchester City	784

Most points amassed by Chelsea over a season

2004/05	95 *	1999/00	65
2005/06	91 *	2001/02	64
2009/10	86 *	2011/12	64
2007/08	85	1997/98	63
2006/07	83	2000/01	61
2008/09	83	1996/97	59
2003/04	79	1992/93	56
1998/99	75	1994/95	54
2010/11	71	1993/94	51
2002/03	67	1995/96	50

* Champions

Average points per season

Manchester United	83.15
Arsenal	72.45
Chelsea	**70.10**
Liverpool	66.70
Leeds United	57.67
Blackburn Rovers	57.00
Newcastle	56.50
Aston Villa	54.45
Tottenham	54.30
Manchester City	52.27

TITLE WINS

Manchester United	12
Arsenal	3
Chelsea	3
Blackburn Rovers	1
Manchester City	1

BANNERS

'CHARLIE COOKE FOR PRIME MINISTER'

FA Cup final, 1970

GAME OF THE DECADE: THE 1900s

Chelsea 9–2 Glossop North End, Division Two, 1 Sep 1906
New signing 'Gatling Gun' George Hilsdon announced his arrival
with a 5-goal haul, setting Chelsea on to an all-time highest
scoreline, and promotion to the top flight for the first time.

POWERPOINTS

'When I met them [after the Champions League final in 2004] I
listened for important things for me. They were saying of course
we want to win, and of course we need to win, because when
you want to create one of the best clubs in the world, you need
to win.

'You cannot go into Asia searching for commercial things . . . if
you are a loser. If you want to take supporters from other English
clubs, no victories? – none of that. So they want to create long
term one of the best clubs in the world and for that they need
short-term victories.

'Peter Kenyon told something important for me: "We don't
want to win one championship, we want to win the first, but we
want to build Chelsea into one of the best clubs in the world."

'They showed me a Powerpoint presentation with numbers . . .
supporters in the world, supporters in England, Man United, Real
Madrid, Barcelona; where Chelsea was, what Chelsea needs to do
in sports terms to push all the other things. And I have got that
responsibility in my hands.

'After that I told them and I showed them my Powerpoint
presentation about my ideas about the team, and they were open
for that. I could show them my way to win, my profile of players,
of teams, of concepts, and they understood it well and we shared
opinions and it was a nice two days.'

**How the Chelsea hierarchy interviewed José Mourinho . . . and
how he interviewed them**

PRIZE MONEY

1914/15 FA Cup runners-up: £725.
2001/02 FA Cup runners-up: £1,675,000.

PSYCHIC

'Standby for the floodgates to open.'

BBC 5Live commentator Alan Green, at the moment Chelsea went 2–0 down, having been reduced to ten men, away to Barcelona in the 2012 Champions League semi-final second leg. The Blues went on to draw 2–2 and win the tie

CONVERT

On 29 June 1930 Stamford Bridge was temporarily transformed into a cathedral by the Bishop of London and tens of thousands of believers celebrating High Mass on the hallowed turf ahead of the fourth Anglo-Catholic Congress, held at the Royal Albert Hall the following day.

NAUGHTY NORRIS

The new Chelsea's massive ambitions were threatened in 1907 by a proposal from Fulham chairman Henry Norris to merge the geographically separate Southern and Football Leagues into a new National League. Norris had summarily rejected a move to the new Stamford Bridge stadium in 1905 and resented the fact a more successful neighbour had sprung up as a result. His plan would have been a setback for the promotion-chasing Pensioners. The proposed merger would have meant Division Two (where Chelsea then played) being split in two along north/south lines, with a *three-year* moratorium on promotion from 1907/08. Naturally the dynamic young Chelsea board were fierce opponents, and the *Chelsea FC Chronicle* published passionate letters of disapproval from supporters. Thankfully, the merger idea was postponed (and later dumped) and as the 1906/07 season played out, Chelsea in any case gained entry to the top tier as runners-up.

ROY BENCH-LEY

Roy Bentley was the English national side's first ever substitute, replacing Chelsea team-mate Billy Gray at outside-right in Switzerland for England 'B' in January 1950.

PURPLE PROSE

'[Willie] Foulke's face when the referee pointed to the centre was a study. Transferred to canvass, labelled "Amazement", it would be the picture of the season at next year's Academy exhibition. What he thought would fill a volume – in several languages.'

Chelsea FC Chronicle

GLAMOUR CLUB

French new wave actor Jean-Paul Belmondo was present at the Parc des Princes stadium to watch Chelsea beat his team Paris Saint-Germain 3–0 in 2004. Related work: *Les Misérables* the movie, 1995.

GAME OF THE DECADE: THE 1910s

Chelsea 2–1 Derby County, Division One, 15 Nov 1913
This was the debut for Chelsea's first foreign superstar, the Great Dane, Nils Middelboe. He was made skipper for the day and was voted man of the match, beginning the Chelsea support's long affection for overseas players.

EASTER BUNNIES

Chelsea believed they had been relegated in 1915 by finishing 19th in Division One, one point and one place from safety. However, thanks to an anonymous letter sent by 'Football King' to a leading sports newspaper, a match-fixing scandal, involving Liverpool and Manchester United the previous Easter, was exposed. An FA hearing established that losers Liverpool had been nobbled by a betting syndicate and United (who had finished 18th) were stripped of the two points earned, saving Chelsea from relegation.

CLUB CONTACTS (1905)

Telegram: 'CHELSTAM, LONDON'
Telephone: '1476 KENSINGTON'

EYE ON THE BALL

Striker Bob Thomson, signed from Croydon Common in 1911, only had one eye. Recalling the legendary Peter Cook and Dudley Moore sketch about the one-legged man auditioning for the part of Tarzan ('a role which traditionally involves the use of a two-legged actor'), it was said Chelsea manager David Calderhead asked, 'How do you manage, Bob, when the ball comes to you on your blind side?'

'I just shut the other eye – and play from memory' was his reply. Despite this disability Thomson thrilled supporters and weighed in with 25 goals in five official seasons – plus 100 more in 'unofficial' campaigns during the First World War.

PEP TALK

'Today we can make history and become champions of England.'
The words Eidur Gudjohnsen used when it was his turn to make the rallying cry before kick-off. Bolton away, April 2005

LETTERS OF NOTE

'In the event all went well. Chelsea lost their first match against the Bulgarian Army team 1–2, but won the second 2–0 against the leading Bulgarian civilian club. Both games were reasonably clean; there were no unpleasant incidents such as marred last year's match between the English and Bulgarian Under 23s, and the crowd in the stadium behaved well. Chelsea spent the time between the two Sunday matches training and resting at Varna, where they were the guests of the Bulgarians at one of the best hotels. I had them all in to drinks after the last match (without any Bulgarians) and they made a good impression on all who met them. The management and most of the team seemed to have been well briefed by someone (? by our department) about the realities of life in Bulgaria and had not been unduly taken in by the VIP treatment accorded them. They had no complaints except about the food (even the best Bulgarian hotel food is pretty disgusting) but there seems to have been little fraternisation; no formal banquet was organised after the matches and none of my staff were invited to attend any social function by the Bulgarians as we were after the Under 23s match last year. This was of course all to the good.

Yours ever, Richard Speaight'

From the UK Foreign Office, in relation to Chelsea's cold war-era tour of Communist Bulgaria in 1958

FIRST MENTION OF CHELSEA

Anglo-Saxon king Offa of Mercia held a synod in AD 787 at Cealthye, generally accepted as modern-day Chelsea.

SHINE

'If candlelight is kind to the human face, then floodlighting certainly lends a magic to a football arena.' Thus wrote a newspaper reporter remarking on the first use of floodlights at Stamford Bridge in 1957. Each set of lamps stood on tubular steel towers reaching up 170ft – almost as tall as Nelson's column. There were six of these erected, despite protests from a few locals about the eyesore, and a total of 288 lamps burning nearly half a million watts.

LET'S CALL THE WHOLE THING OFF

Some reasons for late postponements or abandoned matches:

29 December 1962. Chelsea v Luton Town. One of 26 English matches called off because of tundra-like conditions. The 'big freeze' endured, and the Blues' next league match was not played until 9 February 1963.

29 January 1969. Chelsea 2–0 Preston North End. Called off when a fire in a newly installed electrical junction box caused power failure.

20 January 1972. Chelsea 2–3 Norwich City. League Cup semi-final abandoned with five minutes remaining (and City holding a three-goal aggregate lead) because of blanket fog.

24 January 1976. York City 0–2 Chelsea. Rumours of floodlight failure at Bootham Crescent proved unfounded, but many supporters were put off going.

8 December 1993. Chelsea v Wimbledon. Postponed because structural debris was blowing around the stadium.

23 October 1997. Tromsø 3–2 Chelsea. Blizzards caused this second round UEFA Cup Winners' Cup in the Arctic Circle to be stopped several times for the pitch to be cleared to reveal its markings.

9 December 2003. Besiktas 0–2 Chelsea. The start of the second half was delayed for almost ten minutes so that an avalanche of toilet rolls thrown by Turkish fans could be cleared from the neutral Auf Schalke Arena pitch.

GAME OF THE DECADE: THE 1920s

Corinthians 4–4 Chelsea, Friendly, 4 July 1929
Chelsea become the first English professional side to play in São Paulo, and delight a huge Brazilian crowd with a thrilling comeback, earning the nickname 'the team of the turn'.

RIGHT NEIGHBOURLY

While the rest of Britain froze under blizzards and sub-zero temperatures of March 1965, Chelsea prepared for the FA Cup clash with Peterborough almost as normal. How? Through the generosity of rivals Arsenal, who had been approached by Blues manager Tommy Docherty to use the indoor training centre adjacent to Highbury, and agreed. Chelsea were thus able to turn the heat on the Posh, and won 5–1.

SHED LOADS

It is widely recorded that the 'Shed' roof over the old 'kop' south terrace was built only after greyhound racing arrived at Stamford Bridge, and more for the benefit of that sport's adherents than football's. The idea of cover for that area was first mooted four years earlier, however, in 1928. Stadium landlord and Chelsea director Joe Mears aimed to raise £40,000 by setting up a new company that would own and maintain the stadium. Mears hesitated and the organisation did not materialise; instead the Greyhound Racing Association effectively took over the ground in 1932.

THERE'S AN AWFUL LOT OF CHELSEA IN BRAZIL

Chelsea have fielded more Brazil-born players (eight) than any other in the Premier League: Emerson Thome, Mineiro, Juliano Belletti, Deco, Alex, Ramires, David Luiz and Oscar. Manchester City and Middlesbrough have used six, Arsenal five and Manchester United four.

MOURNING THE PENSIONER

'It will be a pity, if, in dropping the Pensioner, Chelsea in the process mislay that endearing quality of theirs to behave like a more than normally temperamental Mr Punch, bobbing up when he is least expected to give some resounding whacks to Cup-holders and Champions.

'And even if they, in their turn, achieve so exalted a status, they may find themselves regretting the old unregenerate days when the charm of a visit lay in the uncertainty of what would happen there.'

The Times, 27 September 1952, on Ted Drake's decision to pension off Chelsea's long-held nickname in favour of 'the Blues'

GRATUITOUS MENTION OF DAVID BECKHAM TO INCREASE SALES MASSIVELY

Infamously, David Beckham's surname was mis-spelled 'Beckam' on the back of his shirt when he came on as a substitute during Chelsea's 1–1 Charity Shield draw with Manchester United at Wembley in August 1997 (a 4–2 loss on penalties).

Seven months earlier our club had made a more significant contribution to his life story. The midfielder had equalised Gianfranco Zola's early opener in the Premier League game at Chelsea's home in February 1997, a match which also ended 1–1. Afterwards, in the players' lounge under the East Stand, Beckham was approached by pop impresario Simon Fuller who introduced the footballer to a member of a band he managed – 'Posh' from the Spice Girls. That slightly awkward Stamford Bridge meeting blossomed into one of the great celebrity romanc . . . (do I really need to write more? No? Good.) Victoria was obviously a well brought up young lady, otherwise we might now be pondering which club Stamford Beckham should sign for.

Incidentally, Chelsea's (and England's) assistant physio at the time was Terry Byrne. He would later become Beckham's personal manager. Presumably his duties included ensuring the surname was not mucked up again!

NUMERICAL ADVANTAGE

When Chelsea toured Argentina in 1929 the locals were impressed by the tourists' latest innovation – numbers on the backs of their shirts. The press instantly dubbed them 'Los Numerados' – the Numbered Ones. Chelsea had pioneered this aid to player identification, with outfield players wearing numbers 2 to 11 as a trial against Swansea Town on 25 August 1928 (Arsenal wore them the same day in Sheffield against The Wednesday).

'The 35,000 spectators were able to give credit for each bit of good work to the correct individual,' reported the *Daily Express*, 'because the team were numbered, and the large figures in black on white squares enabled each man to be identified without trouble.'

'I fancy the scheme has come to stay,' predicted the *Daily Mirror*. 'All that was required was a lead and London has supplied it.' However, it would be a further ten years before numbered shirts were universally adopted by the Football League.

IN PRAISE OF 'PERCY'

There was considerable outcry from supporters at Drake's decision to ditch the Pensioner badge in 1952. One correspondent, Charlie of Chelsea, noted 'all of us local Chelsea supporters have regarded Percy the Pensioner as our mascot. He has saved us from relegation a few times.' Another, a Mr G.H. White of Greenford, commented, 'I have seen every game at Stamford Bridge since Chelsea started. We are mighty proud of the old boys of Chelsea Hospital and proud to have their picture on our programme. Let Ted Drake produce players like George Hilsdon, Jimmy Windridge and the like to make the name of the Pensioners respected.'

'The next thing,' railed M.N. Rayfield of London, 'will be stopping the old Pensioners from enjoying their privilege of seeing the game free.' In fact, to this day the club still invites the scarlet-jacketed veterans along on matchdays.

COEFFICIENCY

In reverse order, these are Chelsea's coefficient figures, allocated by UEFA in order to rank the teams contesting their trophies in the ensuing season.

2003	7.3330 (25th highest in Europe)
2001	9.0830 (13th)
2002	10.7855 (11th)
1999	16.7185 (16th)
2006	17.7610 (14th)
2010	22.5856 (3rd)
2004	22.7125 (20th)
2009	25.0000 (2nd)
2005	25.1385 (20th)
2000	26.2500 (14th)
2011	26.6714 (3rd)
2007	28.4860 (7th)
2008	30.8985 (1st)
2012	33.0500 (3rd)

PLAYER OF THE DECADE: THE 1910s

Vivian Woodward 27/11/1909 – 28/4/1915

Chelsea's acquisition of England's amateur skipper 'Jack' Woodward in 1909 stunned football and indicated how much Chelsea had grown in just four years. Universally admired for his qualities as a forward and gentlemanly approach, Woodward joined a front five already boasting fellow England stars Hilsdon and Windridge. An architect by trade, oozing class from every wool-clad pore, blessed with physical and mental deftness, Woodward was a talismanic presence. Typically, though, when duty called in 1914 he was one the first to sign up, becoming a Lieutenant in the 17th Middlesex, the 'Footballers' Battalion'. He was on leave having been injured on the front when the Pensioners reached our first FA Cup final in 1915, but waived his slot in the line-up in favour of ever-present Bob Thomson. Woodward was a proper gent who later served as a club director until July 1930.

116 appearances, 34 goals.

WHAT SPECTATORS WANTED (1971)

Spectator references:
All terraces covered
Low-price bench seating
Restaurant facilities
Club car parking facilities
More licensed premises
Other activities

Spectator suggestions:
Improved entrances and exits
Stands closer to the pitch
Covered stands and terraces
Improved toilets
Electronic scoreboard
Pre-and post-match entertainment
Supporters' and social facilities
More season ticket facilities
Boys' enclosures and entrances
More low-price bench seating
Direct link to underground

Results of 1971 survey by stadium developers Darbourne &
Darke.

THE GREAT DANE

It was Vivian 'Jack' Woodward who diverted the 'Great Dane' Nils Middelboe from his intended football destination, Newcastle, to Stamford Bridge. The two had become friends after meeting in successive Olympic football finals of 1908 and 1912 while representing Denmark and England (Middelboe was the first player ever to score a goal in that competition). Such was the reputation of this tall, elegant midfielder with the ground-gobbling stride, that he was handed the captaincy before his debut and pronounced man of the match afterwards. A fixture of the Chelsea side when his banking duties permitted, Middelboe became the first overseas superstar of English football. He continued to play for the Pensioners throughout the First World War, before returning to Denmark, where he resumed the affair with his other football lover, KB of Copenhagen. Every now and then, as a director, he was able to set up friendlies between the two teams, and his descendants visited Stamford Bridge as recently as 2010. During their stay they donated the ball Nils was handed as man of the match on his Chelsea debut to the Chelsea Museum.

GAME OF THE DECADE: THE 1930s

Chelsea 1–1 Arsenal, Division One, 12 Oct 1935
The biggest crowd in English football history at the time – 82,905 – watched the London derby as Irish centre forward Joe Bambrick opened the scoring, only for the Gunners to equalise in the second half.

DERBY DAUBED

Prisoners from nearby Wormwood Scrubs clearing Queens Park Rangers' plastic pitch ahead of Chelsea's visit on Boxing Day 1981 made a remarkable discovery. Straddling the halfway line beneath the thick layer of snow was a message, painted in 4ft high white letters, protesting: 'PERRY BUCKLAND IS INNOCENT'. Teenager Buckland had been found guilty of murdering student Ian Alexander at an Anti-Nazi League disco in 1979, and a campaign to overturn the verdict enjoyed its most daring publicity stunt yet. The match went ahead and Chelsea won 2–0. Green paint applied to disguise the graffito could not prevent the slogan being visible to TV viewers, and it was widely discussed. Buckland remained locked up, though, and later served part of his sentence at Ford Open Prison. There, on the football field graced by George Best, he impressed enough to play for the Prison XI, and even earn a trial at Portsmouth.

THEY'RE NOT LAUGHING NOW

Willie Foulke, who befriended the great George Robey – the 'Prime Minister of Mirth' – in 1905, may have been the first to forge the Chelsea/showbiz connection. It often proved a double-edged sword. Norman Long was a music hall performer who in 1933 recorded a song about dreaming of 'The Day That Chelsea Went and Won the Cup', the scornful lyrics of which are faithfully related here:

Now a little while ago I dreamed a most amazing dream.
It tickled me to death when I woke up.
Now you know just how impossible the things we dream of are –
Well I dreamt that Chelsea went and won the Cup.

Of course as a result of an astounding thing like this,
A host of other strange events occurred.
All folks and things were opposite to what they really are
And the happenings were really quite absurd.

On the day that Chelsea went and won the final,
All the universe went off the reel.
Great Sir Harry Lauder used a five-bob postal order
To stop his shoe from rubbing on his heel.

The sun came out in Manchester and funny things like that,
Jack Jones, M.P., played golf and wore a kilt and Winston's hat,
And a pigeon hatched a guinea pig and blamed it on the cat,
On the day that Chelsea went and won the Cup.

On the day that Chelsea went and won the final,
Farmers all admitted trade was grand.
Lady Astor's bonnet had a Guinness advert on it,
And Jack Hylton ran a chamber music band.

Landlords called round and begged to do repairs galore,
But their tenants said this wasn't fair unless the rents were more,
And a film star had the self-same wife he had the day before
On the day that Chelsea went and won the Cup.

Two motorists collided and each said the fault was his,
And each one said I was doing 50 then.
But the traffic policeman said, 'Oh no' 'twas he who was to blame,
And assessed the speed at something under ten.

In a London pub a person found a hop inside his beer
And the thing is in Fleet Museum yet.
Billingsgate Fish Market was the place for Oxford talks
And gave off a gentle smell of mignonette.

On the day that Chelsea went and won the final
Taxi men had change for half a quid.
And schoolboys – holy Moses – washed their ears and blew their noses
And even used a hankie when they did.

All steaks at boarding houses were as tender as a corn,
A navvy said 'Dear me!' when he sat down upon a thorn,
And De Valera put a statue of Jim Thomas on his lawn
On the day that Chelsea went and won the Cup.

On the day that Chelsea went and won the final
Not a single trav'ler said, 'Oh quaint,'
Phone girls woke from slumber and a man obtained a number
That he asked for in the spring of '28.

Lawyers told the truth and then refused to take their fee,
Twenty folks got OBEs and seven got TTed,
And a sergeant-major shouted, 'Gentlemen, please stand at ease'
On the day that Chelsea went and won the Cup.

Doctors wrote prescriptions that we all could understand,
Post got drunk and eels got stewed and lofters all got canned,
And Gordon Richards wore Carnera's trousers in the Strand
On the day that Chelsea went and won the Cup.

TWITTER YE NOT

'Didier Drogba's newest fan. Holy shitballs.'
US actor Danny DeVito, having watched Drogba net the winner against Barcelona, 18 April 2012

THE SHED END TRIBES

'Any End reflects the area it is in, even one like The Shed, with half London as its cachement [*sic*] area. Thus there are heads at Chelsea, a lot of them in fact, and if you want a brief glimpse of what street fighting men would look like, go and have a look at The Shed, where the beards weigh in alongside the smooth boys. Chelsea's main strength, however, is the in the coffee bars, skin pubs and discos of south London, where a blue and white Chelsea scarf is an almost obligatory part of the local fashion. Croydon, Wandsworth, Modern [*sic*, Morden], Richmond, Brixton, Catford, Wimbledon, these are all Chelsea areas, as well as a hefty stretch going North of the river through Acton, Chiswick Paddington, as far as Kilburn, which has more football allegiances than races. Even North London keeps to the Chelsea fashion, with one actual gang going Chelsea way: the Hendon Shed.'
'Football Gangs', Chris Lightbown, *Time Out*, 1972

DRESSING UP

The early 1990s was the heyday of the Chelsea crowd donning fancy dress for the last away trip of the league season. Pockets of fans still maintain the tradition, but these were the most memorable:

11 May 1991: Aston Villa – Beachwear, surf shorts, Hawaiian shirts.

2 May 1992: Everton – Harry Enfield-style 'Scouser' moustaches, curly wigs, 'calm down' arm movements.

8 May 1993: Sheffield United – flat caps (whippet optional).

30 April 1994: Manchester City – Blues Brothers suits, shades, pork pie hat.

NEW BROOM

'At long last there appears to be the making of a "new" Chelsea, a Chelsea that will not be the butt of music-hall comedians or the despair of London football fans. Mr William Birrell, the Scotsman who is the ex-Queen's Park Rangers manager, who has taken over the managership of the Stamford Bridge club, has been able in the summer season to start the campaign rolling for the creation of a new spirit towards football, and a new attitude by the public towards the club, at Chelsea. If you mention the word psychology he will probably ask what you are talking about, but the fact remains that he is out to make jokes about Chelsea completely unfashionable.'

Hull Daily Mail, **August 1939**

Over 13 war-interrupted years Birrell managed 96 wins in 290 matches, a win percentage of 33. He did, however, bring the 1945 Football League (South) Cup to Stamford Bridge.

PLAYER OF THE DECADE: THE 1920s

Jack Harrow 9/12/1911–20/2/1926
Photographs of this faithful servant of the Fulham Road invariably capture him at full stretch, clearing the adversaries' threat or lying prone after a bone-shattering challenge. Jack was the John Terry of his generation, the full-back putting his body on the line and snuffing opponents out. He performed the same throughout 14 years of near ever-presence. Acquired from Croydon Common, he retired aged 37 in 1926 as the first Chelsea player to play more than 300 times for his club, many as skipper. He remained at the Bridge as third team trainer and coach until moved on by Billy Birrell in 1939.

334 appearances, 5 goals.

ROYAL AZZURRI

Few foreign countries have enjoyed as close a bond with Chelsea as Italy. Many émigrés arriving in London adopted the club because of the shirt – the same colour as their national side. During the Second World War after Mussolini's downfall in 1943, groups of captured Italian prisoners were regularly seen at Stamford Bridge. In Italy itself Chelsea is arguably the most widely admired English club. Three of the club's most successful coaches have been from that country. Gianluca Vialli won the FA Cup, UEFA Super Cup and League Cup in 1998; Carlo Ancelotti brought the first league and FA Cup Double to Stamford Bridge in 2010; and Roberto Di Matteo stepped up from the assistant role to lead the Blues to FA Cup and Champions League glory in 2012.

Here are some of our *azzurri* from down the years.

Carlo Ancelotti	2009	Manager
Gabriele Ambrosetti	1999	Player
Marco Ambrosio	2003	Player
Angelo Antenucci	2000	Coach
Fabio Borini	2007	Player
Pierluigi Casiraghi	1998	Player
Carlo Cudicini	1999	Player
Sam Dalla Bona	1999	Player
Giorgio Ciaschini	2009	Assistant coach
Valerio Di Cesare	2001	Player
Luigi La Sala	2010	Opposition scout
Roberto Di Matteo	1996	Player, assistant manager, manager
Bruno Demichelis	2010	Assistant manager
Giovanni Mauri	2010	Fitness coach
Christian Panucci	2000	Player
Giorgio Pellizzaro	2000	Goalkeeping coach
Luca Percassi	1998	Player
Antonio Pintus	1998	Fitness coach
Claudio Ranieri	2000	Manager
Jacopo Sala	2007	Player
Roberto Sassi	2000	Fitness coach
Gianluca Vialli	1996	Player, player-manager
Gianfranco Zola	1996	Player

WHY CHELSEA FANS FIRST WENT TO MOW

Why did Chelsea supporters adopt the nursery rhyme 'One Man Went To Mow'? The man responsible was Mickey Greenaway, better known for his raucous chanting of 'Zigger Zagger'. Greenaway had followed the Blues since the 1950s and, working for British Rail, travelled home and away, including overseas tours. In Sweden, 1981, he had found a children's tape cassette of songs en route and began playing it in bars before matches for a laugh. His rendition of 'One Man Went To Mow' caught on, though, and was gradually adopted wherever Chelsea fans gathered back home. It has been sung ever since. Greenaway was a hugely popular and influential figure. When he died in 1999 a collection among supporters paid for his headstone in Hither Green cemetery.

COLD WAR WARMTH

At the Café Royal reception following the riotous Chelsea versus Moscow Dynamo friendly in November 1945, the Russians declared that the crowd – which swamped the stadium and hugged the pitchside – had been 'very nice', but that the noise of rattles was something strange to them. Having handed a posy to each of their Chelsea counterparts prior to kick off, at the dinner they invited Chelsea to play in Moscow and passed on a further friendship gift in the shape of white enamelled badges sporting a blue 'D', topped by a red star.

YOU HAVEN'T SEEN ME, RIGHT?

When he launched a vivid new goalie's kit in 2008, Petr Cech revealed the science behind his colour choice. The fluorescent orange distracted strikers, according to 'studies', and inclined them to shoot straight at him.

'This colour is like a sort of alarm or alert which really spreads and is very difficult to avoid, so this should be good for me.' In 2012 Liverpool's keeper Pepe Reina explained his new green strip was like camouflage, as with 'bright colours, attackers see you. Green is like going undercover.' Well they can't both be right.

COCK CROW

In December 1919, a veteran of the First World War, unable to speak since a shell exploded in close proximity to him on the field of battle, was taken to the Bridge to watch Chelsea's derby with Arsenal. In the 35th minute something magical happened. When Harry Ford crossed from the right wing and Jack Cock scored, the war veteran, swept up in the celebrations, suddenly broke two years' silence and loudly acclaimed the opening goal. Chelsea went on to win 3–1 – the first time a game between the two had been settled by more than a one-goal margin – and the old soldier's parleying was fully restored.

GAME OF THE DECADE: THE 1940s

Chelsea 3–3 Moscow Dynamo, Friendly, 13 Nov 1945
One of the most talked-about exhibition matches of all time, this was a diplomatic draw between the cream of the Russian and English games, and Stamford Bridge was swamped by a horde of 100,000-plus spectators.

KIRBY YOUR ENTHUSIASM

Chelsea's first chairman, Claude Kirby, invented Arsenal's iconic white-sleeved strip. While playing golf in the early 1930s he was impressed by the look of a man in white long-sleeved shirt and contrasting sleeveless sweater. He presented the idea of white-sleeved, blue-bodied shirts to fellow board members at Chelsea, but support was not forthcoming. Arsenal acquaintances liked the idea, though, and switched to white sleeves in 1933.

LOVE & HATELEY

Tommy Docherty brought highly-rated centre forward Tony Hateley from Aston Villa to Stamford Bridge in October 1966 with a club record £100,000 heading to the Midlands in exchange.

Hateley's goal also earned the club's first ever FA Cup final appearance at Wembley. It is worth remembering those details before going to see the Doc's brilliant after-dinner act. Two of his best gags involve the former striker. Hateley's passes were so poor, Docherty says, that they were labelled 'to whom it may concern.'

When it wasn't working out for Hateley at Chelsea, Docherty attempted to induce bids from rival managers, including Liverpool's Bill Shankly. During a eulogy about the misfit, Docherty claimed he said to Shanks, '£100,000 wouldn't buy him!' 'Aye,' replied Shankly, 'and I'm one of the 100,000.'

Poor Tony was sold off after just one season: to Liverpool, for £96,000.

HOLD THE LINE

Straight after helping Chelsea win the Premier League and FA Cup 'Double' in 2010, Michael Ballack was disappointed to be told his contract would not be renewed at Stamford Bridge. The news was broken over the phone by manager Carlo Ancelotti.

'This is not how I wanted it,' admitted the sympathetic Italian, 'and I will tell you the story when I see you. Where are you right now?'

'In Florida,' replied the German midfielder.

'Whereabouts?' queried Ancelotti. Ballack gave the name of his hotel.

'But I'm in the hotel next door!' said the Blues manager. 'I'll be over in a minute.' Yards apart, 4,000 miles from London, the two settled down to an evening of convivial discussion.

PLAYER OF THE DECADE: THE 1930s

Hughie Gallacher 30 Aug 1930 – 3 Nov 1934

His stay was relatively brief (four and a bit seasons) but the impact of Hughie Gallacher's performances on those who witnessed them was immortal, beginning with a stunning brace in a 6–2 mauling of Manchester United. A pocket battleship centre forward with lightning feet and endless ingenuity in finding the route to goal, the success recorded on the back pages was hampered only by the turbulence recorded on the front. Divorce, 'foul language' or bankruptcy competed with delight at his crowd-pleasing skills and, sadly for the superstar Scot, it was the news columns that eventually came to dominate. His return to former club Newcastle drew what is still a record crowd for St James' Park, and it was on Tyneside in 1957 that this troubled soul ended his own life on a railway line.

144 appearance, 81 goals.

SEEING THINGS

Files released in July 2012 by the Ministry of Defence and National Archives revealed that a police officer reported seeing a UFO in the sky above Stamford Bridge on Wednesday 10 March 1999. This was the evening of Chelsea's sixth round FA Cup replay against Manchester United, which ended in a 2–0 defeat. There is no truth in the rumour the unidentified flying object was the ball from one of Bernard Lambourde's defensive clearances.

WEMBLEY WIZARDS

It is difficult to overestimate the impact on the Scottish psyche of the football game that took place on 31 March 1928 when 80,000 were packed into the Empire Stadium, Wembley, for the clash with hosts England that day. Among the flower of Scotland on the pitch were Chelsea's hard-as-nails full-back Tommy Law, Alex Jackson (a stylish winger), and devastating centre forward Hughie Gallacher. The 'skill, science and trickery' displayed by the Scots raiders proved irresistible, Jackson hitting a hat-trick in a 5–1 win. Without scoring, Gallacher also sealed his reputation as the cleverest forward in Britain. Chelsea's board would never forget and in 1930, on achieving promotion, hired Jackson and Gallacher. In the posh seats for the 1928 spectacle, with their country on the brink of civil war, were King Amanullah and Queen Sourita of Afghanistan (another of their majesties' engagements was a visit to the GWR works at Swindon, so it wasn't all glamour). Scotland, though, crowned their own royalty that day.

THE KHAKI FINAL

'[Bob] Thomson, the dashing centre forward, had dislocated his elbow at Bolton on the previous Wednesday week, but his arm had made so much progress that it was decided to risk including him in the [FA Cup final] team. He walked on the field with a well-bandaged elbow, determined to lead his colleagues as usual. The spirit was willing but the flesh was weak, and I do not hesitate to say that, whatever chance Chelsea might have had to bring the Cup down south after an interval of fourteen years, they threw it away when they left out Vivian Woodward and gave the place to the player who had figured in every round. I know, too, that Woodward, who was an interested spectator of the match, though quite ready to play, was sincerely desirous that Thomson should retain his position. As matters turned out it was an unfortunate choice.'

Daily Express, 26 April 1915, pondering Lieutenant Woodward's return from the trenches, and Chelsea's 3–0 defeat by Sheffield United in the 1915 final at Old Trafford

COURT IN THE ACT

January 1908. Tommy Miller, first team coach, drunk and disorderly, fined 5s.

OLYMPIC GOAL

At a meeting in Birmingham on Saturday 22 September 1906, Chelsea owner Gus Mears managed to discuss with King Edward VII the offer he had tabled to stage the 1908 Olympic Games track and field in London at Stamford Bridge. The Italian city of Naples was supposed to host the event but in April 1906 an eruption from Mount Vesuvius devastated the city and a new location was sought. His Majesty was sympathetic and said he would definitely attend, but in the event White City Stadium, Shepherd's Bush, was purpose-built for the Games.

ILLUMINATING

The first occasion on which artificial shadows were cast during a match on the Stamford Bridge turf was in March 1957, during a youth team game, a few days before a friendly against Sparta Prague, from what was then Czechoslovakia. Chelsea were relative latecomers to football's postwar floodlighting revolution, but no strangers to the concept. In fact the club's first match under electric light had been on 28 June 1929 in Rio de Janeiro, Brazil, against a combined Carioca XI.

'Chelsea drew 1–1 after a brilliantly contested game,' enthused a Chelsea director to *Athletic News*.

Can your readers picture a cloudless sky all day, with the thermometer at 90 degrees in the shade, then darkness at 6pm and this wonderful city illuminated with millions of lights. We were all entranced and our drive to the ground was full of interest.

The home team were fine players, the goalkeeper performing excellently (all these South American custodians are as good as the very best in England) and their left wing gave a splendid exhibition. The whole team, in fact, were speedy, controlled and trapped the ball magnificently, and took up positions admirably.

Their fault was precisely that of our own side – the forwards dribbled and manoeuvred in front of goal until they were robbed.

The crowd was most sportsmanlike, cheering us to the echo – quite a novel experience for us on this trip – and they let off rockets, squibs and detonators when the play pleased them. Everyone seemed pleased with the result.

RIGHT TRACK

Between 1928 and 1932, on any given Wednesday or Saturday night, the air around Stamford Bridge would be thick with fumes and the ears of spectators filled with the roar of motorcyclists racing around the oval cinder patch surrounding the football pitch. Imported from Australia, dirt-track was soon popularised by the likes of team captain Gus Kuhn, Noel Johnson and even female contestants such as Miss Fay Taylour. The home team,

Stamford Bridge Pensioners, who raced in royal blue, suffered at least one fatality when rider Charlie Biddle was tragically killed at a meeting in May 1928. They won the Southern League from 1929 to 1931, and the National League in 1932, after which landlord Joe Mears abruptly evicted them in favour of more lucrative greyhound racing.

LONG TIME RETIRED

The longest-lived Chelsea player is believed to be Benjamin Howard Baker, the celebrated amateur goalie of the 1920s, who died aged 95 in 1987. Winger Douglas Smale (born March 1916) passed away aged 89 in 2006. At the time of writing there were several former players in their late eighties.

Baker was born a stone's throw from Goodison Park in 1892 to a successful wholesale chemist, and joined the family business – remaining an amateur sportsman throughout his sporting life.

He excelled as an athlete, twice competing in the Olympics at high jump and triple jump; in 1920 he finished sixth in the former and eight in the latter. Perhaps unsurprisingly, his party piece was to kick light bulbs out of ceiling lamps.

While turning out for the Pensioners, he remained available for amateur outfit the Corinthians and the England national side. In later years he humorously recalled being tasked during matches with bouncing the ball around the penalty area, basketball-style, while a Chelsea director barked orders to the outfield players through a loud-hailer.

ILLICIT LAGERS IN BLACKPOOL

It's spring 1965 and under the guidance of young manager Tommy Docherty, Chelsea have bagged the League Cup, bowed out in the semi-final of the FA Cup, and are in with a chance of the league title. Then eight players – Barry Bridges, Joe Fascione, George Graham, Marvin Hinton, John Hollins, Eddie McCreadie, Bert Murray and Terry Venables – were caught defying a midweek curfew summarily imposed by the Doc and sent home . . .

Chelsea's last hopes of an historic second title win went south with those first teamers. Without them the Blues lost 6–2 at Burnley and would finish third, five points behind champions Manchester United. A statement released by the eight players sent home said:

> Shocked at the publicity this matter has received, we feel we should put the whole into perspective. We admit to being out after hours. We were out until 2am and, in that we admit to a breach of club discipline. We think it would have been fairer to us if the manager had made it clear why we were disciplined instead of allowing everyone to draw exaggerated conclusions. What happened was this. We got in at 11pm and then we were chatting in one of the rooms. After half an hour we walked down to the bowling alley and sat around one table, drinking lager. Some of the lads were hungry, so we decided to have a meal. We left the restaurant and returned to the hotel, arriving there at 2am. Mr Docherty was waiting for us. None of us was drunk, nor was there any disturbance. All this time we were together, and there were no girls in our company. Having thought the matter over, we are still baffled why the manager should have felt it necessary to impose such a drastic public punishment when any other club in the country would have dealt with it privately and probably with a fine. This has been a long hard season and perhaps the strain and tension of keeping the club at the top was behind the manager's action. He is a man of snap decisions, who obviously could not see his way clear to relent. We intend to ask the chairman [Mr Joe Mears] for the opportunity of discussing everything with him before we see the manager again. We are sticking together.

500

Frank Lampard is the most expensive Chelsea player to have made 500-plus appearances. In fact he is the only one who cost anything: the rest – Ron Harris, Peter Bonetti, John Hollins and John Terry – all emerged through the club's youth ranks.

LONDON LANDMARKS

Chelsea became the first team in London ever to win the League Cup in 1965, and were the capital's first club to lift the Champions League, formerly the European Cup, in 2012.

ADIEU DROGBA

Didier Drogba's parting message to team-mates on the tactical board at Cobham in June 2012 was 'Blue till I die', followed by his signature, written in permanent ink. Blue permanent ink, of course.

SKIPPERS

It is difficult to provide an accurate record of the players who captained Chelsea before the war – the information was often simply not noted down. However, there are some things we can say. The man who led the Pensioners in the team's first ever FA Cup final was Fred Taylor in 1915. The youngest player to be handed the captaincy was John Hollins, aged 18 years and three months, in the 4–0 League Cup win v Notts County of October 1964; Ray Wilkins was handed the role permanently in April 1975 at just four months older. In 1967, aged 22, Ron Harris became the youngest to lead a team in an FA Cup final at Wembley. The man who has worn the armband more than any other is also the club's most successful skipper: John Terry.

Postwar captains of Chelsea

John Harris	Ken Armstrong
Len Goulden	Derek Saunders
Willi Steffen	Stan Wicks
Tommy Walker	Peter Sillett
Danny Winter	John Mortimore
Roy Bentley	Frank Upton
Bobby Campbell	Frank Blunstone
Bill Dickson	Stan Crowther
Stan Willemse	Ron Tindall

Johnny Brooks
Bobby Evans
John Sillett
Jimmy Greaves
Andy Malcolm
Bobby Tambling
Ken Shellito
Terry Venables
John Hollins
Ron Harris
Tommy Harmer
Joe Kirkup
Tony Hateley
Tommy Baldwin
Marvin Hinton
Eddie McCreadie
Alan Birchenall
David Webb
Peter Bonetti
Peter Osgood
Keith Weller
Steve Kember
Ray Wilkins
Duncan McKenzie
Micky Droy
Ian Britton
Gary Locke
Steve Wicks
John Bumstead
Colin Pates
Tony McAndrew
Dennis Rofe
Clive Walker
Colin Lee
Joe McLaughlin
Joey Jones
Nigel Spackman

Peter Nicholas
Graham Roberts
Dave Beasant
Erland Johnsen
Andy Townsend
Dennis Wise
Vinnie Jones
Paul Elliott
Mal Donaghy
Gavin Peacock
Mark Hughes
Ruud Gullit
Eddie Newton
Steve Clarke
Frank Leboeuf
Gustavo Poyet
Dan Petrescu
Gianfranco Zola
Marcel Desailly
Graeme Le Saux
Jody Morris
Chris Sutton
John Terry
Frank Lampard
Jimmy Floyd Hasselbaink
Carlo Cudicini
Eidur Gudjohnsen
William Gallas
Wayne Bridge
Claude Makelele
Michael Ballack
Ashley Cole
Joe Cole
Didier Drogba
Petr Cech
Florent Malouda

GAME OF THE DECADE: THE 1950s

Chelsea 1–0 Wolverhampton Wanderers, Division One, 9 Apr 1955
The game that sealed the Blues' first title win. Stan Cullis' side were killed off by a late penalty, awarded for hand ball and blasted in by full-back Peter Sillett in front of 75,043 delirious fans.

MY WORD!

'Number eight, Baldwin . . . Osgood . . . And he's scored! Osgood has done it. That was a beautiful shot – I thought it had gone wide, but he picked his spot and Osgood's now kneeling down, and just waving at the crowd, and so after 38 minutes Osgood has made it two.'

BBC TV's Kenneth Wolstenholme on Peter Osgood's winning strike against Real Madrid in the 1971 UEFA Cup Winners' Cup

THE ROAD TO MUNICH (1)

Chelsea's tenth Champions League campaign began with some familiar opponents. When the balls were drawn from the bowl for the group stage the Blues found themselves in Group E along with new signing Juan Mata's former side Valencia and onetime kaiser of Stamford Bridge Michael Ballack and his Bayer Leverkusen side, runners-up in the Bundesliga. By January there would be a further connection as Kevin de Bruyne was hired from the fourth club, Belgian champions Genk. André Villas-Boas steered his team to a perfect three wins, with 10 goals for and none against. Travelling results were less impressive: draws at Genk and Valencia, and then defeat in Germany. Drogba gave an early indication of his intent, though, with a powerful display and two goals in the 3–0 win over the Spaniards at the Bridge that made the Blues group winners. The only other English club to make it through to the knockout phase was Arsenal – the two Manchester clubs succumbing early.

TEMPER TEMPER

There has been no drinks machine in the visitors' dressing room at Stamford Bridge for several years – not since a frustrated set of Spanish players smashed it up after a Champions League defeat.

BALL BOY PIONEER

Chelsea were innovators in the use of boys to fetch balls shot wide of the goal. One of the very first was James Ridley, 13 at the time, who lived at 7 Stamford Road (later renamed Holmead Road), a few doors down from the Rising Sun, directly opposite Stamford Bridge. Young Jim answered a call put out locally for youngsters to work at matches and there are photographs of him on duty at the Pensioners' second home game against West Brom on 23 September 1905. One photo was presented to him as a memento.

The story goes that Chelsea hired the lads in order to emphasise the size of Willie Foulke in goal. 'To see him run, scattering the mud and water to right and left, was a sight for the gods,' wrote the *Blackpool Gazette* of 'Little Willie'. The 6ft 2in 23-stone keeper would sometimes playfully carry the boys off the field under his arms at the final whistle; he was certainly known to carry young supporters off the field in that fashion.

Proximity to his sporting heroes had a long-lasting effect on Jim, who joined the 17th Middlesex – the so-called Footballers' Battalion – when the First World World War broke out in 1914. Unfortunately he was captured at Cambrai in 1917 and was kept prisoner of war until peace returned. Despite the experience he lived a long life and remained a lifelong Chelsea fan, fond of recalling serving alongside former players such as Vivian Woodward and 'Pom Pom' Whiting, right up to his death in 1975.

THE THOROUGHLY NICE
CHAP IN THE BLACK

We all know that referees receive a lot of stick – some of it justified. However, honourable mention should be made of two men in black with regard to handling Chelsea games in a fair fashion. The man who has officiated more wins for the Blues than any other is Mike Dean (2001–12), with 30. However, two other refs have overseen a higher percentage of Chelsea victories than Mr Dean's 67 per cent.

They are Alan Wiley (1999–2010) with 26 wins, 72 per cent of all games; and Steve Bennett (2001–10) with 26 wins, 68 per cent. Sadly both are now out of the English game.

Unlamented by the Fulham Road End faithful was the retirement of Chorley's Jack Kelly. Between 1957 and 1961 he refereed six Chelsea games, all defeats, including 4–2 and 3–2 losses to Spurs, a 4–4 draw and a 3–0 loss to Arsenal, a 3–1 defeat by Leicester, and a 2–0 loss to West Brom. Other generations had cause to fear the names of G.C. Denton (1931–7) with 8 defeats, 80 per cent of matches in charge); R.J. Burgess (1949–51), 4 defeats, 100 per cent; Frank Cowen (1953–68) 5 defeats, 71 per cent; and David Allison 1985–94, 6 defeats, 75 per cent.

Since you ask, 1994 FA Cup final arbiter David Elleray's record in Chelsea matches was 10 wins (40 per cent), 8 draws (32 per cent) and 7 losses (28 per cent).

CHELSEA CUP FINALS
RANKED BY ATTENDANCE

Leeds United 2–2 Chelsea
Sat 11 Apr 1970
FA Cup, Wembley
Att: 100,000

Tottenham Hotspur 2–1 Chelsea
Sat 20 May 1967
FA Cup, Wembley
Att: 100,000

Stoke City 2–1 Chelsea
Sat 4 Mar 1972
League Cup,
Wembley, Att: 100,000

Chelsea 2–0 Millwall
Sat 7 Apr 1945
Football League (South) Cup,
Wembley, Att: 90,000

Manchester United 0–1 Chelsea
Sat 19 May 2007
FA Cup, Wembley
Att: 89,826

Everton 1–2 Chelsea
Sat 30 May 2009
FA Cup, Wembley
Att: 89,391

Liverpool 1–2 Chelsea
Sat 5 May 2012
FA Cup, Wembley
Att: 89,102

Portsmouth 0–1 Chelsea
Sat 15 May 2010
FA Cup, Wembley
Att: 88,335

Chelsea 2–2 Man United
Sun 9 Aug 2009
FA Community Shield,
Wembley, Att: 85,896
(Chelsea won 4–1 on penalties)

Chelsea 1–3 Charlton
Sat 15 Apr 1944
Football League (South) Cup,
Wembley, Att: 85,000

Chelsea 1–3 Manchester United
Sun 8 Aug 2010
FA Community Shield,
Wembley, Att: 84,623

Chelsea 1–1 Manchester United
Sun 5 Aug 2007
FA Community Shield,
Wembley, Att: 80,731
(United won 3–0 on pens)

Manchester United 4–0 Chelsea
Sat 14 May 1994
FA Cup, Wembley
Att: 79,634

Middlesbrough 0–2 Chelsea
Sat 17 May 1997
FA Cup, Wembley
Att: 79,160

Aston Villa 0–1 Chelsea
Sat 20 May 2000
FA Cup, Wembley
Att: 78,217

Middlesbrough 0–2 Chelsea
Sun 29 Mar 1998
Coca-Cola Cup, Wembley
Att: 77,698

Middlesbrough 0–1 Chelsea
Sun 25 Mar 1990
Zenith Data Systems Cup,
Wembley, Att: 76,369

Arsenal 2–0 Chelsea
Sat 4 May 2002
FA Cup, Millennium Stadium
Att: 73,963

Chelsea 1–1 Manchester United
Sun 3 Aug 1997
FA Charity Shield, Wembley
Att: 73,636
(United won 4–2 on pens)

Liverpool 2–3 Chelsea
Sun 27 Feb 2005
Carling Cup, Millenium Stadium
Att: 71,720

Arsenal 1–2 Chelsea
Sun 25 Feb 2007
Carling Cup, Millennium Stadium
Att: 70,073

Bayern Munich 1–1 Chelsea
Sat 19 May 2012
UEFA Champions League,
Allianz Arena, Munich
Att: 69,901
(Chelsea won 4–3 on pens)

Manchester City 4–5 Chelsea
Sun 23 Mar 1986
Full Members' Cup, Wembley
Att: 67,236

Chelsea 2–0 Manchester United
Sun 13 Aug 2000
FA Charity Shield,
Wembley, Att: 65,148

Leeds United 1–2 Chelsea
Wed 29 Apr 1970
FA Cup (replay), Old Trafford
Att: 62,078

Arsenal 1–2 Chelsea
Sun 7 Aug 2005
FA Community Shield,
Millennium Stadium, Att: 58,014

Chelsea 1–2 Liverpool
Sun 13 Aug 2006
FA Community Shield,
Millennium Stadium
Att: 56,275

Sheffield United 3–0 Chelsea
Sat 24 Apr 1915
FA Cup, Old Trafford
Att: 49,557

Real Madrid 1–1 Chelsea
Wed 19 May 1971
UEFA Cup Winners' Cup,
Karaiskakis Stadium, Piraeus
Att: 45,000

Chelsea 1–2 Everton
Sat 8 Aug 1970
FA Charity Shield,
Stamford Bridge, Att: 43,547

Chelsea 3–0 Fulham
Sat 26 Apr 1919
Victory Cup, Highbury
Att: 36,000

VfB Stuttgart 0–1 Chelsea
Wed 13 May 1998
UEFA Cup Winners' Cup,
Stockholm, Att: 30,216

Leicester City 0–0 Chelsea
Mon 5 Apr 1965
League Cup (second leg),
Filbert Street, Att: 26,957

Real Madrid 1–2 Chelsea
Fri 21 May 1971
UEFA Cup Winners' Cup
 (replay),
Karaiskakis Stadium, Piraeus
Att: 24,000

Chelsea 3–2 Leicester City
Mon 15 Mar 1965
League Cup (first leg),
Stamford Bridge, Att: 20,690

Real Madrid 0–1 Chelsea
Fri 28 Aug 1998
UEFA Super Cup,
Stade Louis II, Monaco
Att: 9,762

Chelsea 3–0 Newcastle United
Wed 14 Sep 1955
FA Charity Shield,
Stamford Bridge, Att: 12,802

CHELSEA'S 'BOOT ROOM'

By summer 2012 18 former Blues players of the Premier League era had become managers of various league or international teams, including Chelsea. In July 2012 Gus Poyet shed some light on why so many of those in the 1990s moved into the dugout: 'The place we went to the most was the masseur's room at the training ground at Harlington. In the morning, an hour or an hour and a half before training, the main group was always there, talking about football situations or problems or fixtures. We would sit around the table that someone was having a massage on. It wasn't a spectacular room, but it was one of the best rooms I've ever been in in football.'

MY WORD!

'Zola's first touch. Intervention. Wise . . . and Zola's through! Ohhh, that is a goal worthy of winning any cup final in the world! Gianfranco Zola's second touch has sent the Chelsea fans wild. One of the most dramatic substitutions in European cup final history . . .'
TV's Ian Darke describing substitute Gianfranco Zola's winner against Stuttgart in the 1998 UEFA Cup Winners' Cup final

PURPLE PROSE

'Together they proceeded to kick the match half dead, rifle its pockets and scatter the loot of a dreadful game into the night air.'

Daily Express, Chelsea v Roma, 1966

TACTICAL TED

'We played [a friendly in December 1959] in Bilbao where it was so muddy you couldn't kick a ball more than ten yards and Ted Drake, who was a wonderful motivator but not a great tactician, decreed "no pass-backs". Anyway, I get hold of the ball about ten yards inside our half and Reg Matthews in goal calls for it. So I turned round and wellied it and all you could hear was Reg yelling, "Bloody 'ell" as it flew over his head into the net for the only goal of the game. All the boys burst out laughing. I was laughing until I looked over and saw Ted's face. The only tactic he'd thought of and I'd scuppered it. I was a hero in Spain, however. When we went out on the town that night I wasn't allowed to buy a single drink.'

Former full-back John Sillett

GAME OF THE DECADE: THE 1960s

Sunderland 0–1 Chelsea, Division Two, 18 May 1963
Tommy Docherty's aggressive tactics – and a goal off veteran Tommy Harmer's nether regions – earned a decisive win against Chelsea's main promotion rivals, stunning a triumphalist Roker Park.

THAT NEW BROOM THING . . .

'Mr Leslie Knighton, who is to be secretary of Chelsea F.C. immediately the present football season ends, has a reputation for finding youngsters and creating players out of them. With Chelsea's money and his own astuteness Mr. Knighton should not be long in making Chelsea a formidable force.'

Knighton was secretary-manager from August 1933 to April 1939, with a win percentage of under 40 per cent, and highest finish of eight in Division One.

PURPLE PROSE

'[Marvin] Hinton swept up stray passes with the nonchalance of a man spiking litter in the park.'

The Times, 1 May 1967

THE RUUD BOY

'When he came into the side, along with Mark Hughes [in 1995], he was one of the first big steps forward – bringing in class players to make the club better. As a player he had a great presence: great athlete, very strong, dominating. Arrogant, if you like, but in a good way because all the good players are arrogant. He was always more concerned about his own group: he didn't bother too much about the opposition. His philosophy was that if we had the ball then the opposition could do what they liked because they would be chasing the ball.'

Steve Clarke on Ruud Gullit, 2005

KERRY OLÉ

In April 1991 the struggling might of Real Madrid, newly managed by Radomir Antić, almost became the temporary quarters for popular goal-getter Kerry Dixon. He would have partnered Emilio Butragueño in place of Hugo Sánchez at the Bernabéu – quite something to have on one's CV. In the event, the loan request was turned down by Blues boss Bobby Campbell. Dixon scored four times in the last five games of the season as Chelsea finished eleventh; over in Spain, Real finished third.

CHELSEA CROWDS AT
STAMFORD BRIDGE ABOVE 64,000

Chelsea 1–1 Arsenal	12/10/1935	Div 1	82,905
Chelsea 3–1 Swindon	13/10/1911	FA Cup	77,952
Chelsea 3–3 Blackpool	16/10/1948	Div 1	77,696
Chelsea 0–4 Tottenham	16/10/1920	Div 1	76,000
Chelsea 2–2 Arsenal	9/10/1937	Div 1	75,952
Chelsea 1–0 Wolves	9/4/1955	Div 1	75,043
Chelsea 1–5 Arsenal	29/11/1930	Div 1	74,667
Chelsea 0–3 Birmingham	4/3/1931	FA Cup	74,365
Chelsea 1–1 Arsenal	3/4/1953	Div 1	72,614
Chelsea 1–3 Arsenal	22/4/1933	Div 1	72,260
Chelsea 2–0 Man Utd	4/3/1950	FA Cup	70,362
Chelsea 1–1 Arsenal	17/1/1947	FA Cup	70,257
Chelsea 0–0 Cardiff	5/3/1927	FA Cup	70,184
Chelsea 2–0 Tottenham	8/1/1964	FA Cup	70,123
Chelsea 2–1 Newcastle	27/12/1929	Div 1	70,000
Chelsea 2–1 Aston Villa	2/4/1920	Div 1	70,000
Chelsea 3–0 Fulham	21/1/1939	FA Cup	69,987
Chelsea 1–1 Fulham	10/2/1951	FA Cup	69,434
Chelsea 2–5 Stoke	12/10/1946	Div 1	67,935
Chelsea 1–3 Tottenham	15/4/1960	Div 1	67,819
Chelsea 4–2 Aston Villa	4/10/1947	Div 1	67,789
Chelsea 0–4 Tottenham	30/9/1933	Div 1	67,454
Chelsea 3–3 West Brom	2/10/1954	Div 1	67,440
Chelsea 0–0 Arsenal	1/11/1947	Div 1	67,277
Chelsea 0–0 Southampton	3/2/1923	FA Cup	67,105
Chelsea 4–0 Swindon	31/1/1920	FA Cup	67,054
Chelsea 1–1 Man Utd	13/4/1906	Div 2	67,000
Chelsea 1–1 Middlesbrough	27/12/1921	Div 1	67,000
Chelsea 1–2 Aston Villa	30/1/1960	FA Cup	66,671
Chelsea 3–6 Man Utd	2/9/1959	Div 1	66,579
Chelsea 0–1 Stoke	11/5/1963	Div 2	66,199
Chelsea 0–0 Arsenal	26/10/1957	Div 1	66,007
Chelsea 0–2 Tottenham	14/10/1950	Div 1	65,992
Chelsea 1–1 Arsenal	27/12/1954	Div 1	65,922
Chelsea 2–0 West Ham	26/1/1946	FA Cup	65,726
Chelsea 2–2 Arsenal	28/4/1934	Div 1	65,344

Chelsea 0–1 Aston Villa	9/2/1946	FA Cup	65,307
Chelsea 1–2 Aston Villa	21/3/1913	Div 1	65,000
Chelsea 1–0 Cardiff	25/2/1922	Div 1	65,000
Chelsea 3–1 Newcastle	28/1/1950	FA Cup	64,664
Chelsea 3–0 Charlton	26/3/1937	Div 1	64,463
Chelsea 4–2 Arsenal	15/10/1938	Div 1	64,443
Chelsea 2–1 Arsenal	21/11/1931	Div 1	64,427
Chelsea 2–2 Man City	26/3/1948	Div 1	64,396
Chelsea 1–1 Arsenal	12/10/1935	Div 1	82,905
Chelsea 3–1 Swindon	13/10/1911	FA Cup	77,952
Chelsea 3–3 Blackpool	16/10/1948	Div 1	77,696
Chelsea 0–4 Tottenham	16/10/1920	Div 1	76,000
Chelsea 2–2 Arsenal	9/10/1937	Div 1	75,952
Chelsea 1–0 Wolves	9/4/1955	Div 1	75,043
Chelsea 1–5 Arsenal	29/11/1930	Div 1	74,667
Chelsea 0–3 Birmingham	4/3/1931	FA Cup	74,365
Chelsea 1–1 Arsenal	3/4/1953	Div 1	72,614
Chelsea 1–3 Arsenal	22/4/1933	Div 1	72,260
Chelsea 2–0 Man Utd	4/3/1950	FA Cup	70,362
Chelsea 1–1 Arsenal	17/1/1947	FA Cup	70,257
Chelsea 0–0 Cardiff	5/3/1927	FA Cup	70,184
Chelsea 2–0 Tottenham	8/1/1964	FA Cup	70,123
Chelsea 2–1 Newcastle	27/12/1929	Div 1	70,000
Chelsea 2–1 Aston Villa	2/4/1920	Div 1	70,000
Chelsea 3–0 Fulham	21/1/1939	FA Cup	69,987
Chelsea 1–1 Fulham	10/2/1951	FA Cup	69,434
Chelsea 2–5 Stoke	12/10/1946	Div 1	67,935
Chelsea 1–3 Tottenham	15/4/1960	Div 1	67,819
Chelsea 4–2 Aston Villa	4/10/1947	Div 1	67,789
Chelsea 0–4 Tottenham	30/9/1933	Div 1	67,454
Chelsea 3–3 West Brom	2/10/1954	Div 1	67,440
Chelsea 0–0 Arsenal	1/11/1947	Div 1	67,277
Chelsea 0–0 Southampton	3/2/1923	FA Cup	67,105
Chelsea 4–0 Swindon	31/1/1920	FA Cup	67,054
Chelsea 1–1 Man Utd	13/4/1906	Div 2	67,000
Chelsea 1–1 Middlesbrough	27/12/1921	Div 1	67,000
Chelsea 1–2 Aston Villa	30/1/1960	FA Cup	66,671
Chelsea 3–6 Man Utd	2/9/1959	Div 1	66,579
Chelsea 0–1 Stoke	11/5/1963	Div 2	66,199

Chelsea 0–0 Arsenal	26/10/1957	Div 1	66,007
Chelsea 0–2 Tottenham	14/10/1950	Div 1	65,992
Chelsea 1–1 Arsenal	27/12/1954	Div 1	65,922
Chelsea 2–0 West Ham	26/1/1946	FA Cup	65,726
Chelsea 2–2 Arsenal	28/4/1934	Div 1	65,344
Chelsea 0–1 Aston Villa	9/2/1946	FA Cup	65,307
Chelsea 1–2 Aston Villa	21/3/1913	Div 1	65,000
Chelsea 1–0 Cardiff	25/2/1922	Div 1	65,000
Chelsea 3–1 Newcastle	28/1/1950	FA Cup	64,664
Chelsea 3–0 Charlton	26/3/1937	Div 1	64,463
Chelsea 4–2 Arsenal	15/10/1938	Div 1	64,443
Chelsea 2–1 Arsenal	21/11/1931	Div 1	64,427
Chelsea 2–2 Man City	26/3/1948	Div 1	64,396

MY WORD!

'Osgood, now Hutchinson, Cooke . . . and Osgood heads the goal! Brilliantly scored by Osgood! Charlie Cooke the man who made it, Osgood running on the blind side of the defence, guiding the ball with his head, sending the goalkeeper the wrong way . . . and the Chelsea fans have suddenly erupted.'

BBC TV's Kenneth Wolstenholme describes
Peter Osgood's 1970 FA Cup final equaliser

RELICS OF THE SHED

The old Shed wall, which stands opposite the megastore and tours entrance at Stamford Bridge, is the last remnant of the original 1905 stadium, but not quite as it now appears. The first 30ft of it used to be buried beneath mud banking, and fans climbed up terraces to stand and watch from the very top where it is painted blue; the soil was excavated in 1994 during redevelopment. Shed-enders between the 1960s and 1980s were known as the loudest of all Chelsea fans. One section of the terrace would regularly try to out-sing others with a rendition of 'We're the white wall . . . (middle . . . or west side) of the Shed!' The modern Tea Bar café is named in honour of the shack at the back of the stand where Sheddites could get their fix of hot Bovril or Waggon Wheels.

TARBY ON THE WING

Scouse comedian Jimmy Tarbuck once guested for a Chelsea XI in a game against QPR. It was the testimonial in 1968 of full-back (and later youth and first team manager) Ken Shellito, forced to retire through injury.

ACCIDENTAL TOURISTS

Nottingham Evening Post, 17 March 1932: 'Chelsea F.C. Have accepted an invitation to play the Preussen Football Club at Berlin during the Whitsun holidays, probably on Saturday May 14th.'

The Times, 12 May 1932: 'Wild scenes in the Reichstag. Police called to deal with the Nazis.'

The tour went ahead. Chelsea played Bayern in Munich on 15 May, and Preussen in Berlin on the 17th. The only serious doubts raised concerned the German FA's ban on their teams taking the field against professionals.

SOME PLAYERS OF THE MONTH

January 1972	David Webb (Evening Standard)
December 1996	Gianfranco Zola (Premier League)
October 2002	Gianfranco Zola
September 2003	Frank Lampard
November 2004	Arjen Robben
January 2005	John Terry
March 2005	Joe Cole
April 2005	Frank Lampard
October 2005	Frank Lampard
March 2007	Petr Cech
August 2008	Deco
October 2008	Frank Lampard
November 2008	Nicolas Anelka
March 2010	Florent Malouda
March 2011	David Luiz

PLAYER OF THE DECADE: THE 1940s

John Harris 5 Jan 1946 – 7 Apr 1956
A wartime guest from Wolves who lifted the Football League (South) Cup as skipper in 1945, the son of Scottish international Neil signed permanently a few months later when peace finally arrived. An acclaimed full-back and leader of the Pensioners throughout his time at the Bridge, Harris was also hard as nails. When Ted Drake was considering a switch to Chelsea as manager, it was Harris and Roy Bentley whose brains he picked during a long round of golf. Drake arrived in 1952 and converted Harris to a half-back role, judiciously making way for Peter Sillett, such a key figure in the 1954/55 title win. The following season, aged 39, Harris quit to take up managerial roles, notably at Sheffield United, before leaving football to become a lay preacher. He died aged 71 in 1988.

364 appearances, 14 goals.

GIVING A TOSS

In the modern era matches are broken down into moments endlessly scrutinised from every angle for the removal of unfairness. In earlier days even some of the most important decisions were left to chance. One of the oddest involving Chelsea came in March 1966. Docherty's side had drawn 3–3 on aggregate with AC Milan in the last 16 of the Inter-Cities Fairs Cup, and a play-off at San Siro had ended 1–1. No more football – the winner would have to be decided by the toss of a coin.

When the German referee, Herr Baumgartner, presented for inspection his deutschmark to the respective skippers – Cesare Maldini for the hosts and Ron Harris for Chelsea – Chopper spotted that one side sported a German eagle and the other the head of man he didn't recognise.

As visitor, Harris was awarded the call. He didn't fancy the eagle, which he felt was 'too Germanic', and instead opted for the head, which, it turns out, was that of Max Planck. In selecting the founder of quantum theory, Chopper chose very wisely.

Chelsea won and progressed to the quarter-finals, enjoying what one newspaper described as 'a beer party in their hotel' – thanks not to a striker or goalie, but a theoretical physicist.

FOULKE ANGLES

When Chelsea's Willie Foulke saved the last-minute penalty of Manchester United's Bob Bonthron in the 0–0 draw on Christmas Day 1905 at Clayton, the forward's manager railed at him for ruining a match-winning gift against promotion rivals. Bonthron retorted that 'Little Willie' was such a colossal presence on the goal line there was 'nowhere left to aim.' Foulke saved ten penalties in his first and only season at the Bridge, including two plucked from the air within minutes of each other against Port Vale.

POLITICAL FOOTBALL

The first African footballer to grace Stamford Bridge in royal blue was Ralph Oelofse, a white man born in Johannesburg in 1926. He flew to England at his own expense in October 1951 and made his debut the following March as a centre-half, making his Chelsea debut in place of Johnny Harris. Oelofse quickly impressed enough for manager Billy Birrell to jet out to SA to look for more of his ilk – despite protests there and in London against the persecution of the black majority.

Oelofse figured in just seven more games before switching to Watford. Others from the same region followed later: Derek Smethurst, Colin Viljoen (capped by England), Roy Wegerle (USA) and the club's first black South African, Mark Stein – whose father Isaiah Stein was actually imprisoned by the apartheid regime in the 1960s. Up to 2012 the following other African countries have been represented at Chelsea:

Cameroon – Geremi
Uganda – Joel Kitamirike
Liberia – George Weah

Democratic Republic of Congo – Claude Makelele and
  José Bosingwa
Ghana – Marcel Desailly and Michael Essien
Nigeria – Celestine Babayaro and John Mikel Obi
Ivory Coast – Didier Drogba and Salomon Kalou

ASSISTANCE IS FERTILE

When Fernando Torres squared the ball to his Chelsea and
Spain team-mate Juan Mata in the Euro 2012 final against Italy,
he helped make history in several ways. Firstly, he set Mata up
to become the first footballer to score on his Premier League,
Champions League, FA Cup and European Championship debuts
for club and country. Secondly, by providing the assist, Torres leap-
frogged Germany's Mario Gomez to win the tournament's Golden
Boot. Prior to that the two strikers were locked on three goals,
with Gomez ahead on assists (one). As a result of his generosity,
Torres matched Gomez and was awarded the prize because he had
accrued his goals over fewer minutes of playing time.

MY WORD!

'Drogba . . . Candela . . . Lampard, Frank Lampard here for
Chelsea – Lampaard! That could be the championship! Frank
Lampard for Chelsea, and they are within touching distance
now. And of all the people to score the goal that could seal the
championship, who else? It's Frank Lampard.'
  **BBC TV's Steve Wilson describing Frank Lampard's first goal in
  the win at Bolton that won the Premier League in 2005**

TRENCHANT WORDS

'You have played one another and against one another for the
Cup; play with one another for England now.'
  **Lord Derby, addressing the teams of Chelsea and Sheffield United
  after the 'khaki final' at Old Trafford, April 1915**

AUF WIEDERSEHEN, GOODNIGHT

When the England national thrashed their Austrian counterparts 6–1 at Cricketer Platz, Vienna, on 6 June 1908, four of the Three Lions' goals derived from the boot of the nascent Chelsea squad; Jimmy Windridge and George Hilsdon each bagging a brace. A further strike came from Vivian Woodward. A little over a year later Woodward switched from Spurs to Chelsea to form a stellar forward line at the Bridge.

NOT ON THE BACK OF THE SHIRT

HYACINTH – middle name of Celestine Babayaro
TUDOR – middle name of Peter Sillett
MOHAMMED – middle name of Frank Sinclair
IKEM – middle name of Eddie Newton
ANDRZEJ – first name of Eddie Niedzwiecki
ERNAN – middle name of Joe Sheerin
LESLIE – first name of Mark Hughes
GEARS – middle name of Stuart Kingsley Whiffen
JAMES – middle name of Frank Leboeuf
TENNYSON – middle name of Derek Kevan
EUCLID – middle name of Clive Wilson
VICTOR – middle name of Bobby Tambling and Jason Cundy
McLEOD – middle name of Glen Johnson
GLENIS – middle name of Michael Gilkes
EARL – first name of Mark Stein
RENATO – middle name of Paulo Ferreira
ADOLF – first name of 'Alf' Hanson
LEVI – middle name of Les Stubbs
ABSOLOM – middle name of Joe Bambrick
GOLCHRIST – middle name of Ron Brebner
PIERRE – middle name of Graeme Le Saux
KJELBDJERG – mis-spelling of Jakob Kjeldbjerg's name that was
    on his shirt for the 1993/94 season only

REPUTATIONS

'It makes a tremendous difference; when the crowd was apathetic and almost silent, it had a demoralising effect on the team; the game became lifeless and players began to wonder how much longer there was to go. In these last few matches the crowd's enthusiasm has made us all very sorry to hear the final whistle, because we have enjoyed the game so much.

'As that roar rolls around the ground it is almost like a hand on your back, driving you forward. You get to balls that seemed out of reach.'

Roy Bentley, hailing the response to manager Ted Drake's demand for more passion at the Bridge, 13 September 1952

UN-WISE

'I used to work in a bank till 3 o'clock and then go to training. I enjoyed it; I couldn't afford just to play football – I used to take home 5k a year. I'd never have had Dennis Wise as a customer.'

Erland Johnsen on his semi-professional days back home in Norway, 1997

BEFORE THERE WAS FOOTBALL

The London Athletic Club's groundsman at Stamford Bridge, Charles Perry, was employed to help lay the cinder track for the first modern Olympics in Athens, 1896.

PREMIER RECEPTION

'I've got to say I was determined to enjoy the day, but when I walked out and got the reception that I got, I had a little choke. That was a good moment. And then when you're walking to the podium and you see the Premiership trophy, the feeling was there. At last! For me to be involved after so long at the club – that was a great moment.'

Steve Clarke, 2005, on Chelsea lifting the league title for the first time in 50 years

BLUE IS THE COLOUR –
EXTENDED VERSION

The songwriters of the legendary Chelsea 1972 anthem 'Blue Is The Colour' were Daniel Boone and Rod McQueen, commercial pop songwriters and performers of the 1960s responsible for Boone's biggest hit, 'Beautiful Sunday'. The rousing club song was released on veteran producer-songwriter Larry Page's Penny Farthing Records label. Page produced several Chelsea songs, including the lesser-known 'Chelsea We Love You'. But nothing compares to 'Blue'.

'I'd looked after bands such as The Kinks, The Troggs, Sonny & Cher etc. and produced many hits including The Troggs' "Wild Thing" and "Love Is All Around",' Page later recalled. 'But I am and always have been a loyal Chelsea fan and came up with the idea of doing a Chelsea song involving the players while sitting in the stands at the Bridge.

'Daniel and Rod, the actual writers of the song, knew nothing at all about football, so I fed them all the details about the ground, colours, etc. We deliberately avoided any players' names so it wouldn't date, although as we know now the ground changed – big time!

'The main vocals that went down were myself and Daniel Boone, and we just "stacked" our voices up in the Marquee studio in the West End. All the players had to do was mime along. So by the time the team came in to Les Reed's studio the job was done.

'Contrary to popular belief it wasn't produced for the 1971/72 League Cup final. As I remember it, I think we played Charlton the week after we recorded it – and got beat.

'I still love to hear it played at the ground every game and was touched to hear the old song was played by a Guards band at Ossie's memorial service.'

'Blue Is The Colour' proved a huge success, peaking at number five in the charts – the first football-related song to reach such dizzy heights. Only two other clubs' anthems have charted higher since – Liverpool's 'Anfield Rap' (1988) and 'Pass And Move' (1996), and Manchester United's 'Come On You Reds' (1994).

Boone and McQueen's classic, re-recorded in various languages in the 1970s, was reconfigured by the Vancouver Whitecaps soccer team in Canada in 1979 as 'White Is The Colour'. Of course, the proper version still rings out on matchdays at Stamford Bridge.

DO THEY MEAN US?

'The Chelsea balance sheet [a profit of £7,000] is a remarkable one. They competed in the Second Division of the League and hence had not such attractive matches as the Arsenal and Tottenham Hotspur. But their ground is the most accessible in London, and they can always command a gate of 30,000. In these circumstances it is surprising that they have not a better team. For a long time last winter they had an excellent chance of finishing at the top of the table, and gaining promotion, but though there were obvious weaknesses, no attempt was made to repair them. Their supporters complained, but still there was no move to get the players required. It was thought that more enterprise would be shown for the coming season, but again no new men of note have been engaged. The most urgent need is a centre forward. Apparently the club are not prepared to pay the price for a first-class man.'

Townsville Daily Bulletin, **27 August 1927**

GAME OF THE DECADE: THE 1970s

Chelsea 2–1 Leeds United, FA Cup final replay, 29 Apr 1970
The most watched club football match in UK history – 28.5m viewers – inspired a generation of Blues supporters as Osgood and, at the death, Webb, saw off the bitter rivals from Yorkshire.

THE SPECIAL FONDANT

Brian Pullman, Chelsea's press conference steward, has been offering biscuits to the club's managers before they step into the room to face the media since the mid-1970s. In 2004, it soon became evident that José Mourinho's biscuit of choice with his coffee or glass of water was the legendary Custard Cream. Brian made sure he never went without, and José gifted him a favourite scarf when he left in September 2007. When 'the Special One' returned to the Bridge in 2010 as boss of Champions League adversaries Inter, Brian ensured that the exquisitely decorated fondant biscuit was in place as usual. He received an affectionate hug – and a new Armani snood – from José in return.

BEFORE THERE WAS FOOTBALL

Stamford Bridge was once a novelty pleasure ground. In November 1901 the newly-formed 'Aero Club of Great Britain' lifted off in a balloon and carried its gentleman members to a height of 10,000ft before landing comfortably at Maidstone, Kent.

A year later an inquest was held into the death of John Tickner, who fell 100ft from the trailing rope of a balloon that had carried the Revd John Bacon and others engaged in a race against some cyclists on the ground. The balloon had suddenly lifted again once people had alighted, and Tickner was dragged to his doom.

A MINOR INCONVENIENCE

The hooligan problem meant that Chelsea supporters were occasionally banned from attending away matches. Dedicated fans always found ways round the problem. One example was Chris Sice and Mark Roberts, both determined to attend Southampton-Chelsea on 22 March 1986 by hook or by crook. Chris recalls:

> Unfortunately the police were rounding up anyone hanging around the ground, and there wasn't anyone selling a ticket. We met another straggler who tagged along. Things looked bleak until we spotted the front door to one of the stands was ajar. We could see the outside broadcast truck from the BBC and slipped into the stand, hiding in the cubicle of a ladies toilet. Carefully removing the light bulb, two of us stood on the cistern, and the other took the seat so no-one could detect us. Unfortunately, we had three hours to kill: in the dark, in the loo, with a complete stranger – and none of us able to say anything in case we got found out.

My word it was worth it, though. Come 2.45, one by one we slipped out, spotted a posse of families of the Chelsea players, sat with them and sang up for the Blues. When Colin Pates scored for us to win 1–0, you saw the familiar pockets of Chelsea fans going up all around the ground.

As the t-shirt under my bomber jacket said, 'You can't ban a Chelsea fan.'

BIG BAND TEL

One of the most original and memorable Chelsea goal celebrations came during the 8–0 title-winning victory over Wigan in May 2010. When he scored, Didier Drogba skipped over to the flag at the corner of the East and Matthew Harding stands, knelt down and pretended to play the guitar for fans. He was soon joined by Florent Malouda (on drums). Of course the team's real drummer was Petr Cech, who guested for a band on live Czech TV in 2012, playing Nirvana covers. It's not clear whether his team-mate Fernando could hear the drums that night.

Drogba loves his music. He has featured on a song released by Wills and the Willing in 2007 ('Skin', with Michael Essien, a fundraiser for the CLIC-Sargent charity), sung with the band Magic System for the Ivory Coast team's official single, and made a cameo appearance on the video of Julia Channel's 2012 dance tune, 'Forever In A Day'.

But let's skip back half a century or so and uncover 'Chelsea's Sinatra', 17-year-old Terry Venables. Soon after signing professionally East Ender Tel had set up his own company, Terry Venables Ltd, and a new line for his business was singing. Indeed, Venners had always wanted to croon and was under the tutelage of a singing coach on Denmark Street, Soho, when he wasn't being put through his paces by Ted Drake. Still an England Youth international, he would write his own words and 'ask a professional' to convert his humming into melodies. One of his lyrics apparently went: 'Nobody knows, nobody cares/About the world or how it began/I'm the man who invented the moon and the stars/Moon and the sun, starts and the sky.'

By December 1960 Terry had recorded a four-track test pressing and come to the attention of the famous band leader Joe Loss. In turn his musical dalliances became a concern to Drake, especially when the youngster's debut with the Loss Orchestra at the legendary, 2,500 capacity Hammersmith Palais was scheduled for Friday 23 December, the night before a home game against Manchester United. He needn't have fretted overly. 'As Terry is playing the following day,' said the band leader, thoughtfully, 'I'll probably put him on for a short spot at 9.45 in this first appearance.'

How did Drake respond? By dropping Venables. 'Terry has had a lean spell recently,' he claimed, 'and I decided to give him a rest before his singing appointment was made.' Terry-less, Chelsea lost 2–1 and 6–0 in successive matches to United.

OUR KEN

Musings from Ken Bates' column in the Chelsea programme:

'Let me make it quite clear. [Chelsea Independent Supporters Association] do not support the Club, they are not independent and their little association has an extremely small membership. Furthermore they try to make money by competing with Chelsea, all this while seeking recognition, free press tickets on match days and a place at the table for discussions – they have no relevance.'

PLAYER OF THE DECADE: THE 1950s

Jimmy Greaves 24 Aug 1957 – 29 Apr 1961

Jimmy Greaves had already accumulated an astonishing 114 goals in one season before making the first team. When the prodigious teenager made a stunning debut at White Hart Lane on 26 August 1957, one reporter announced: 'Ted Drake has made a rare discovery in this young Londoner, who, with all the assurance of a veteran, slipped into the tempo of a battle waged to the last gasp before 52,580 roaring fans and scored Chelsea's equalising goal.' Just four years later the press were fearing how the Blues would fare without him, such had been his goalscoring prowess in the intervening years. The East Ender is still rated by many the club's greatest home-produced player – two-footed, innately stylish, effortlessly effective. His misfortune was to feature in an era when his goals tally was often matched or exceeded by those conceded by team-mates at the back. Frustrated by a lack of ambition and the salary cap, Greavesie ruefully switched to AC Milan before arriving back in London – at Tottenham.

169 appearances; 132 goals.

THE MAKELELE ROLE

So distinctive was the tidy, mobile, interventionist style of defensive midfielder Claude Makelele, that during José Mourinho's management at Chelsea the phrase 'The Makelele Role' became widespread in football.

'When a manager asks me to come to his team, I say what is my function?' the Frenchman explained in 2006. 'I never change my system when I play. I speak with [Mourinho], I say, "You see me play. My system is this, I play this." He said the system that was in his head, and I say okay, no problem.'

SEASON TICKET PRICES

1906/07
To Ground and Stand
Gentlemen: £1 1s
Ladies and School Boys: 10s 6d

To Ground Only
Gentlemen: 10s 6d
Ladies and School Boys: 5s 6d

1967/68
East Stand block A: £12
East Stand blocks C & F: £18
West Stand centre: £18
West Stand wings: £12
North Stand: £12

2012/13
East Upper: £940 (concessions £440)
East Lower family centre: £595 (£285)
West Lower: £900 (£450)
West Upper: £1,250 (£480
Matthew Harding Upper: £880 (£425)
Matthew Harding Lower: £750 (£380)
Shed End Upper: £880 (£425)
Shed End Lower: £750 (£380)

FLOGGED IN THE PROGRAMME

Bovril: 'Available all round the ground. The Food Beverage beloved by Athletes, and Prominent Footballers find it very useful during their training.' (1906/7)

PLAYER OF THE DECADE: THE 1960s

Bobby Tambling 7 Feb 1959 – 30 Mar 1970
In a decade of stellar performers, one statistic stands out: all-time highest Chelsea goalscorer with 202 strikes. Supported by his direct, distinctive running at pace and enterprising dribbles, the left-footed Storrington boy's effectiveness in front of goal was legendary. Though the two were often at loggerheads he suited new manager Tommy Docherty's methodology well, exploiting the ball played quickly into forward channels and rarely missing games. Assuming the mantle abandoned by Greaves, he netted his first hat-trick in September 1961; it was to be one of eight, including five against Villa in September 1966. Bobby played for England three times and scored the Blues' first FA Cup final goal at Wembley in 1967. But in January 1970, when Dave Sexton was looking for different qualities up front, he was sold to Crystal Palace.

366 appearances, 202 goals.

FLOGGED IN THE PROGRAMME

Oxo: 'Your famous OXO is always used by our Team. When in training they prefer it to all other fluid beefs.' (1911/12 handbook)

'MEARS OUT'

Brian Mears, great-nephew of the club's founder, Gus, was ousted as chairman in May 1981 following dramatic supporter action at Stamford Bridge during the last game of the 1980/81 season. Fans had brought banners calling for his head because of problems with the team and the club's coffers, and constantly chanted the same 'Mears Out!' refrain. The visitors were Notts County, needing a win to reach the First Division for the first time in 55 years.

Midway through the second half, with County holding a two-goal lead, the mutinous mood spilled angrily onto the pitch. Chelsea supporters invaded the field, holding up their protest banners and halting play. Scores of police, six on horseback, attempted to restore order. Eventually the field was cleared and the game rumbled to a close before further abuse of Mears greeted the final whistle. Mears later recalled:

> When we played the last match against Notts County, I had spittle all over me from up above in the East Stand, which I had helped build. People were spitting at me, shouting at me, throwing things at me. [Wife] June was devastated. I said: 'This is it. I'm finished.' June replied: 'You're absolutely right, love. We can live our lives better than this.'

FLOGGED IN THE PROGRAMME

Owbridge's Lung Tonic: 'Damp Ground, Cold Winds . . . football spectators run greater risks than players.' (1909/10 handbook)

PLAYER OF THE DECADE: THE 1970s

Peter Osgood 16 Dec 1964 – 8 Sep 1979

The inscription on the statue outside Chelsea's stadium reads: 'Stamford Bridge has many heroes but only one king.' That captures the transcendent power of Ossie, who is the only player so far to have been immortalised in that way on the Fulham Road. As does the fans' song about him, still sung today, about a star coming out of the Shed and bringing great times to the Blues. A centre forward of swagger, attitude and style, he scored vital goals in the 1970 FA Cup final replay against Leeds and the UEFA Cup Winners' Cup final and replay with Real Madrid the following year – truly iconic victories. To many, with his King's Road lifestyle he also encapsulated the swinging sixties era and when he was transfer-listed in 1971 supporters started a vigil until he was reinstated. Fittingly, glamorous actress Judy Geeson came out of a nearby pad to hand out cups of tea. A big man in every sense, he left a huge gap when another bust-up with Dave Sexton led to his departure in March 1974. His return in December 1978 could not rekindle the magic and it is his golden period of 1970 and 1971 on which that statue was modelled.

376 appearances, 150 goals.

NO HISTORY

Liverpool's record attendance at Anfield in the league is the 58,757 recorded on 27 December 1949, when visitors Chelsea drew 2–2.

AWAY SUPPORT

In the pre-motorway days of the 1940s and '50s fans became used to travelling in numbers to away matches, frequently departing from Fulham Road by coach at midnight for the lengthier away trips. The Chelsea FC Away Supporters Club (the first fan group) was founded before the 1948/49 season by Mr C.G. Barnes, Peter Ralph and others, and arranged such trips as well as the usual social events. Peter remembered the away travel as being great fun and, perhaps surprisingly, lots of women went along. His mother joined him for a jaunt to Derby with the club once – simply for the day out.

Back then a trip to Manchester could take all night and that was not the only quaint element. Peter recalled one coach driver stopping in the early hours of the morning and waking everyone up. 'Look,' the driver announced, 'the famous crooked spire of Chesterfield parish church!'

Later, fans might decide to make the journey to watch the Blues on a whim. A woman at one of the club's 'Alive & Kicking' reminiscence groups recently recalled being part of a bunch in a Fulham pub who did just that. A Friday night lock-in had led to a good old sing-song round the piano, and the prospect of a jaunt to the Midlands proved irresistible. A load of the carousers piled into a Transit van and steamed north, naturally taking the piano with them in the back. The next day one lucky publican in the Midlands was surprised to open his doors to a load of happy-go-lucky Chelsea fans with their own piano. The result of the game is unknown, but the pub did brisk business . . . and the 'old Joanna' was left there as a memento.

GIVE US THE SHIRT

'I was saying in five minutes I'll do much better than you. Five minutes after, bring oxygen and take me to the hospital! But five minutes later, more. You're playing fucking shit.' José Mourinho recollecting his half-time 'threat' to substitute himself and the coaching staff for his underperforming players at Bolton on 30 April 2005. Chelsea scored twice in the second half to clinch the title.

NEVER A TRUER WORD . . .

'Mark me, my son, the name of Chelsea has never been sweet to the ears of those who prophesied and hoped for my failure.'
1909 Chelsea FC handbook

PLAYER OF THE DECADE: THE 1980s

Pat Nevin 13 Sep 1983 – 28 May 1988
The Scottish winger was always *different*. The first truly effective dribbler for a decade, he was also a thoughtful and empathetic individual with a holistic approach to football and fascinating world view. He wrote on indie music for *NME* and *Chelsea News* and went to gigs or art-house films rather than the pub after games. But it was as one third of a brilliant attacking triumvirate with Kerry Dixon and David Speedie that he is most fondly remembered. Polar opposites personally, professionally they were seamless, opening up tight 1980s defences with efficiency and flair. (Dixon might just as easily have been the focus of this piece.)

Promotion was earned in his first season, and creditable successive sixth-place finishes in the top flight, largely down to their chemistry. At the same time he smartly used his special relationship with supporters to challenge the terrace racism of some, to considerable effect. Even when he took one of the worst penalties of all time, against Manchester City, he was instantly forgiven. Seemingly mistrusted by John Neal's successor John Hollins, though, Wee Pat became frustrated and switched to Everton in 1988, much lamented.

237 appearance, 45 goals.

FLOGGED IN THE PROGRAMME

Autoglass: 'Every kid in your street wants to kick the ball as hard as Leboeuf. Now where was it you parked your car?' (2000 programme)

DO THEY MEAN US?

'Is Ranieri felling the pressure? "Peuh!" . . . Claudio's "talking tough!" . . . "If we haven't won the championship in three years . . . I will have failed!" . . . That's the stuff the Chairman wants to hear! . . . expect a robust vote of confidence!

'Ranieri insists he's "not a magician" . . . but if he can't pull a rabbit out of the hat . . . you can bet Ken Bates'll have the little bugger by the scruff of the neck before you can say . . . "it's a game of two halves" . . . which takes about six minutes now Chelsea's new interpreter's whittled it down!

'Why haven't Chelsea got a club magician? . . . They've got everything else! . . . bet they would if Glenn Hoddle was still around! Ho ho! . . . The Saint and the sorceress! . . . isn't it?'

Ron Manager (aka comedian Paul Whitehouse), December 2000

NEVER A TRUER WORD . . .

'In the words of one of the football critics, "Chelsea's was a glorious failure."'

1911 handbook – following a two-point defeat in the race for promotion

FANCY A SWIFTY?

Ben Whitehouse scored the only goal the first time Chelsea hosted Blackburn Rovers in December 1907, and in some record books it is cited as Chelsea's quickest ever.

However, it was actually notched straight after the half-time break, and in the most unusual circumstances. Chelsea's forwards had dominated most of the first half against the Lancastrians, with luxuriously-moustached goalkeeper Bob Evans under considerable physical pressure.

When the teams returned for the second half it emerged Evans needed treatment for injury and was not coming straight back onto the field. Rovers continued with ten men, skipper and right-back Bob Crompton temporarily stepping between the sticks.

It was the Pensioners' kick-off and on a treacherous surface at the Bridge they immediately took advantage of the numerical supremacy, forcing play down the left, where Crompton would have been, towards inside-forward Whitehouse, who struck a shot that easily eluded Crompton and went in off the post. The goal was timed at 13 seconds after the restart.

In any case, Keith Weller took just 12 seconds to find the net at home to Middlesbrough in the League Cup on 7 October 1970.

On 19 August 2012, Branislav Ivanovic scored the quickest opening goal of any Chelsea season at Wigan, timed at 1 minute 48 seconds.

6,000 UP

Chelsea's 6,000th league goal was scored by Frank Lampard against Arsenal at the Bridge on 29 October 2011.

SHIRTY

Players' squad numbers were fixed for the first time at the start of the 1993/4 season. These were Chelsea's Premier League men back then:

1	Dmitri Kharine	19	Neil Shipperley
2	Darren Barnard	20	Glenn Hoddle
3	Andy Myers	21	Mark Stein
4	David Lee	22	Paul Elliott
5	Erland Johnsen	23	(none)
6	Frank Sinclair	24	Craig Burley
7	John Spencer	25	(none)
8	Damian Matthew	26	Andy Dow
9	Tony Cascarino	27	David Hopkin
10	Gavin Peacock	28	Michael Duberry
11	Dennis Wise	29	Anthony Barness
12	Steve Clarke	30	Nick Colgan
13	Kevin Hitchcock	31	Zeke Rowe
14	Gareth Hall	32	Muzzy Izzet
15	Mal Donaghy	33	Terry Skiverton
16	Robert Fleck	34	Craig Norman
17	Nigel Spackman	35	Jakob Kjeldbjerg
18	Eddie Newton		

PSYCHIC

'Dull days in winter are usually muddy days, and I don't see what advantage the spectators would have. The ball would become coated with mud, and be no different to the present ball.' Chelsea's secretary-manager David Calderhead on the proposal to replace brown leather balls with white ones, August 1927.

PENALTY FARE

The highest number of different penalty-takers used over a season was in 1934/35 when five different players tried their luck – Bob McCauley (missed), Willie Russell (scored), Jack Horton (missed), George Mills (missed) and Dickie Spence (scored).

Occasionally two different spot-kickers have been used in the same match. The title-winning 8–0 victory over Wigan on 9 May 2010 featured successful conversions from Frank Lampard and Didier Drogba. Not so fortunate on 27 February 1988 were Kevin Wilson and Micky Hazard, who both spluttered from the spot in a 3–1 defeat at Newcastle United.

Against Portsmouth on 27 December 1983 at the Bridge Kerry Dixon had his first penalty saved by Alan Knight and a second rebounded off the bar. When his next effort against Brighton was also saved, Dixon lost his role as penalty-taker first to Tony McAndrew, then Nigel Spackman, then Pat Nevin. In 1988/9 centre-back and skipper Graham Roberts was successful a remarkable 12 times from 12 yards (his only failure was a save by Sunderland's Tony Norman in March).

Dixon rarely took penalties again, and finished his Chelsea career almost nine years later on 193 goals, just nine goals behind table-topper Bobby Tambling. How many might he have hit, but for that penalty problem back at Christmas 1983?

MY WORD!

'Well he scored a magnificent header to equalise, take it to extra time. He gave away a penalty that should have been advantage Bayern, but wasn't. And it's come down to Drogba, who this time *is* the fifth penalty taker for Chelsea in the final shootout . . . He's done it! The greatest night in the history of Chelsea Football Club! European champions. They've beaten Bayern in their own backyard.'

Sky Sports' Martin Tyler describes Didier Drogba's winning penalty in the 2012 Champions League final shootout

FRANKLY AMAZING

Frank Lampard is the only career midfielder to appear in the top 25 of all-time Premier League goalscorers. More than a fifth of those strikes have come from outside the box – easily the highest proportion among his peers.

STOPPED

When the Blues reached the 1994 FA Cup final, the squad were induced to record a single, 'No One Can Stop Us Now' (available on the *Blue Flag* compilation on Cherry Red Records, since you ask). It is credited to Tony Hiller and Barry Upton, who are manager and performer respectively with 1970s pop legends Brotherhood of Man, and songwriters/producers of some pedigree; Barry also takes the rap for such triumphs as Steps and the Cheeky Girls. Both support Chelsea: Tony shared a box at the Bridge with other Tin Pan Alley stalwarts while Barry married a Russian lady who became an avid fan.

Barry explained that 'No One Can Stop Us Now' was actually the brainchild of a certain well-known agent associated with the Blues at the time.

'It was Eric Hall's idea,' he said in 2007. (Hall was renowned in the 1990s as the larger-than-life 'monster monster' adviser to footballers, and a former music PR man.) 'He was managing Dennis Wise and a few others at Chelsea. And he is also a nephew of Tony Hiller, who was still managing me from the Brotherhood of Man days.' Manager at the time was Glenn Hoddle – himself guilty of crimes against music such as 'Diamond Lights'. As soon as Hoddle's side beat Luton Town 2–0 in the semi-final at Wembley on 9 April 1994, Hall was on to Tony: 'We're in the final. We must have a song released with the team. And we've got to get it out on the streets as soon as possible to get the sales before the match.' The final was only five Saturdays away, and the likes of Woolworths buy in their stock two weeks in advance.

'Tony contacted me the evening of the semi – I was on the way to a gig,' Barry recalled. 'We started talking it through. We wanted something with an "I Love Rock'n'Roll" feel. A bit of "We Will Rock You" wouldn't go amiss either. I had the backing track in my head that night, and coming up on the train the following day Tony had half the lyrics already written.

'By teatime on Sunday we'd laid down the backing track and had the lyrics for "No One Can Stop Us Now". Then we realised – we needed a b-side! We didn't have time for a completely new song, so I took one of my old tracks off the shelf and we wrote a song over that. It was called "We Thank You Sincerely" and was designed as a sort of message from the players to the fans, which was a nice touch.

'Monday lunchtime, and Eric Hall got the players together after training and brought them round to a recording studio near the ground.

My strongest memory is of how difficult it was to teach most of the players like Wisey and Mark Stein this song, and trying to get them to stay in time with the backing, let alone in tune! Most of the black players were into rap and were trying to get that going.

'Eric, typically, was bringing all sorts of outsiders into the studio too: reporters, cameramen, along with a load of Lucozade hats and bottles. It was so annoying, but then I just burst out laughing. It was so absurd. Great fun to do.'

The single was completed on the Tuesday, pressed and distributed in good time. When it charted for the first time, Barry was listening to the countdown on the radio at a barbecue and was delighted. It peaked at number 23.

Unhappily, the title didn't prove prophetic – Man United of course beat us 4–0 at a sodden Wembley.

'What made it slightly worse was that if Chelsea had won we'd have got another week in the charts.'

Three years later, Mike Connaris's collaboration with Suggs, 'Blue Day', managed one place higher. Perhaps the fact that the team had won the cup this time helped, or maybe it was a slightly better song.

ARGYLE SWEATER

When Ted Drake's Chelsea toured the USA in summer 1954 they only had one goalkeeper with them. When Bill Robertson became injured with several of the eight matches still to complete, fellow tourists Plymouth Argyle loaned them Bill Shortt as they had a 'spare'. Shortt clocked up 10,000 air miles as a result, and Chelsea repaid the favour by playing a friendly at Home Park later that autumn.

PLAYER OF THE DECADE: THE 1990s

Ruud Gullit 19 Aug 1995 – 28 Jan 1998
When this Ballon d'Or winner, World Soccer Football of the Year, European Cup, European Championship and European Cup winner made his debut for Chelsea against Everton in 1995 it was, manager Glenn Hoddle drooled, like watching a man playing football among boys. A shock signing, the dreadlocked superstar symbolised (and later spearheaded as player-manager) a brave new dawn for the club, and it is purely as the vital pioneer that he features here. Even at 33 the former Milanista's extraordinary qualities were evident and effective, expanding Chelsea's horizons and almost earning an FA Cup final appearance in 1996 with a powerful header, but for tweaked hamstrings and Manchester United's good fortune to receive a diabolical back-pass. When Hoddle moved to the England dugout in 1996 the charismatic Dutchman became the first democratically elected player-manager in Chelsea's history, so vehement was the stadium chanting in his favour. By the end of his first season in that role the Blues had, unforgettably, won the FA Cup for the first time in 27 years. The end came swiftly and sadly, an argument over his wages – as a player – meaning the club deposed him in favour of a someone he had often sidelined: Gianluca Vialli.

50 appearances, 7 goals.

NEVER A TRUER WORD . . .

'We are sure that none of our supporters will ever forget that memorable last Saturday of season 1911/12. The excitement was intense, and when news came through that Wolverhampton Wanderers had beaten Burnley (the only other Club with a chance of promotion) the sight was such as has never before been witnessed at Stamford Bridge, and probably never will again. The critics who had been so fond of asserting that Chelsea had no following of its own, were forced to admit that they were wrong, as it was proved beyond question that Chelsea has thousands of supporters as loyal and enthusiastic as those of any club in the country.'

1912/13 handbook

STAT'S YOUR LOT

It is now one of the myths carved into the bark of football's ancient oaks that Chelsea are a 'methodical' and somewhat 'dour' team. Yet the Blues side of 2004/5 earned a record 95 points in winning the Premier League that season under José Mourinho, and Carlo Ancelotti's Double-winners set a new high of 103 league goals in 2009/10.

GAME OF THE DECADE: THE 1980s

Sheffield Wednesday 4–4 Chelsea, Milk Cup, 30 Jan 1985
A 0–3 half-time deficit unforgettably transformed by the introduction of winger Paul Canoville into a 4–3 lead, let slip by Doug Rougvie's late howler.

PURPLE PROSE

'Jimmy Greaves – an old head on his shoulders and dynamite in his feet.'

***The Times*, 1958**

HOW TAPPING-UP USED TO WORK

'One day [in 1960] we were coming back on the train from a match up north and West Ham – I can't remember who they'd been playing – were on the same train as us. We all knew each other – you did in those days – and one of the West Ham players, Phil Woosnam I think, came into our carriage and said: "Ron, have you got a minute, can we have a word?"

'We went right up to the end of the train and suddenly there was Phil, along with John Bond, Malcolm Musgrove, Bobby Moore and Ken Brown. "What's going on here?" I thought. Phil asked, "Do you fancy coming to play for West Ham?' I said, "Yes, by all means, but what about Chelsea, or Ted Fenton, West Ham's manager?"

"Don't worry about him," came the reply, "just ask Chelsea for a transfer." So I did.

'Ted Drake, the Chelsea manager, went berserk and the Chelsea board rejected my request. That was that. But then a year later there was a deal set up which meant Andy Malcolm came to Chelsea and I went to West Ham in part-exchange. It was all very above-board in the end.'

Former Blue Ron Tindall

OUR KEN

Musings from Ken Bates' column in the Chelsea programme:

'I refused to move Chelsea to Loftus Road despite the offer of substantial financial inducement and David Dein's uninvited intervention as self-appointed "honest broker" in the dispute between Duggan [of property developers and Stamford Bridge freehold owners Cabra] and myself. After some minutes of ear-bashing I told him to sod off and not interfere in Chelsea's affairs. I don't know if he was on a success fee if he had persuaded me to ground-share but he certainly received a fee of over £40,000 to appear as a so-called expert witness on behalf of Cabra at the Public Enquiry which was part of Cabra's scheme to throw Fulham out of Craven Cottage. When I popped into Fulham Town

Hall unexpectedly to watch proceedings, Dein scuttled out like a frightened rabbit when he saw me.'

JOSÉ'S CHOICE

Imagine you are José Mourinho. It is summer 2004. You are a Champions League winner with Porto, newly installed manager of Chelsea, being chauffeured around London in a limousine, when a call comes on your mobile. You have a choice of striker the club will buy for you: Mateja Kezman, 105 goals in 112 games for PSV, or a wantaway teenage prodigy from Everton who, it's suggested, will light up Euro 2004. You confidently make your decision, and stick with it. Imagine . . .

LAST RITES

On 19 August 1961, during a dull 2–2 home draw with Nottingham Forest on the opening of Chelsea's first season in five without the talismanic striker Jimmy Greaves, a supporter took out a cornet on the terraces and proceeded to play a full, mournful version of 'The Last Post'. The lament effectively sounded the death knell for Ted Drake's ten-year reign at the Bridge, and Chelsea's first title-winning manager was replaced a month later by Tommy Docherty.

FIT TO GRACE THE SHIRT?

In December 1984 Chelsea pulled off something of a coup. The club had been strapped for cash for nigh-on a decade, languishing in Division Two for five years – the longest spell postwar – and three-quarters of the stadium was crumbling.

Then, quite out of the blue, at home to Grimsby Town the name of an airline would appear on the players' shirts for the first time – in English and Arabic.

A few days earlier chairman Ken Bates had announced that Bahrain carrier Gulf Air forked out £150,000 to grace the jersey over the remaining five months of the campaign. The full measure was paid upfront, and the story goes that promotion was supposed to mean sponsorship worth two or three times that amount over seasons to come.

And as stories go, it went – promotion was secured, but for some reason the Middle Eastern bounty failed to materialise. Chelsea's shirts would remain 'naked' for two seasons. Gulf Air soon found themselves threatened and eventually eclipsed by a big new player in Arab airlines, and a future sponsor of the Blues: Emirates.

In 1986 the royal blue was adorned with three successive commercial logos, those of Grange Farm, Bai Lin Tea and Simod. The first two were quite bizarre and all three short-lived. Grange Farm was Bates's personal Home Counties hideaway, producing yoghurts and ice creams ('all ice cream needs some air, otherwise it would set like concrete,' cooed one advertisement, rustically). Bates was fond of bidding football journalists with the delightful farewell: 'Right, I'm off to my 300-acre farm – you lot can bugger off to your council houses.' Grange Farm was worn on the club's own-produced 'Chelsea Collection' kits for just a few matches before making way for Bai Lin Tea.

The brainchild of well-connected fraudster Peter Foster, the Chinese tea's alleged slimming claims were later proved utterly bogus. This was a shock because the product had been endorsed by Page 3 sensation Samantha Fox, tax-evading jockey Lester Piggott and notoriously money-averse Sarah Ferguson – all renowned nutritionists. Foster was later jailed for the fraud. Bates sold Grange Farm in the late 1990s.

Finally, in March 1987, a more substantial sponsor appeared in the form of Italian sportswear firm, Simod, yet again on a short-term deal. Come summer Bates would negotiate a different, £250,000 deal with the Football League for Simod to sponsor the short-lived Full Members' Cup.

Desktop computer and games console pioneer Commodore was a very fashionable and successful brand in September 1987, the month they first signed a three-year shirt sponsorship deal with Chelsea worth a then eye-watering £1.25m: a British football record amount for that time.

'This is a golden day and a new golden era for Chelsea. Glory Days are here again,' Bates had announced – at the start of a season which actually saw the Blues relegated.

Commodore's fate was even worse. A series of disastrous moves led to bankruptcy in April 1994 – the same month Chelsea finally reached the FA Cup final for the first time in 24 years.

Thankfully, since then the fortunes of our shirt sponsors have greatly improved.

1983/84 **Gulf Air** – flag carrier airline of Bahrain, rivalled by Emirates of Dubai from 1985.

1986/87 **Grange Farm** – Ken Bates' private farmland fiefdom, flogged off in 1997.

1986/87 **Bai Lin Tea** – bogus 'slimming aid' peddled by convicted fraudster.

1986/87 **SIMOD** – Italian sports casual clothing and footwear brand.

1987–93 **Commodore** – US-based home computer pioneer, responsible for first desktop computer, the Commodore 64.

1993/4 **Amiga** – early personal computers marketed by Commodore, notably Amiga 500, used mostly for gaming.

1994–97 **Coors** – UK arm of US brewing giant, with Cobra among its modern brands.

1997–2001 **Autoglass** – Bedfordshire-based vehicle glass repair and replacement.

2001–6 **Emirates** – airline arm of Dubai leisure conglomerate, founded 1985.

2005–8 **Samsung Mobile** – phone arm of the South Korea-based multinational since the 1980s.

2008–12 **Samsung** – diverse Korean conglomerate chiefly known for electronics, founded in 1938.

THE GENIUS OF ZOLA

'He just came into the dressing room, if you like, an insignificant little character – and got his gear on. Very polite, said "hello" to everybody. You look at that and say: "You don't get much for your money these days." Because he wasn't very big, he wasn't very imposing. But he suddenly seemed to get bigger on the training pitch. Everything he did was just magic: his first touch was fantastic, his finishing ability was great – not always, mind, I've seen him miss a few. But straight away you could tell you were in the presence of a genius. Fiercely competitive. But always in control of himself. He had controlled aggression. He was not aggressive in the sense he was going to run around tackling people, but aggressive in being fiercely competitive.'

Steve Clarke (2005) on his friend and colleague Gianfranco Zola's arrival at Chelsea in 1996

PURPLE PROSE

'[Peter Osgood] drifts about as silently and elusively as a smoke ring.'

The Times, 1966

PLAYER OF THE DECADE: THE 2000s

Frank Lampard 19 Aug 2001 –
No player over Chelsea's long history has had such a consistent impact on each season of a decade than this unique midfielder. (Surely only John Terry comes close.) Achieving double figures in goals every season from 2003/4 to 2011/12, he also established a record for successive appearances as an outfield player of 164. It is not merely consistency, nor adaptability – adding a new string to his bow each summer through hard work – but flair and insightfulness. For every nerveless penalty dispatched in a semi-final there is a defence-splitting ball for a breakthrough goal, or a sublime finish (as at Barcelona in 2006). For years the name most selected by fans to grace replica shirts, he is a remarkable

ambassador for the Blues, several times the England national side's player of the year, and the highest scoring midfielder of the Premier League era. And still he remains underrated. Adapting to a deeper role in 2012, it was his inventive, perfectly executed pass that rocked Barcelona at Camp Nou en route to the 2012 Champions League final. And it was he who captained the team to glory in the final, the greatest night in the club's history.

522 appearances, 186 goals (and counting).

OUR KEN

Musings from Ken Bates' column in the Chelsea programme:

'If the Football Association had taken heed of my urgent request earlier this season [1985/6] and installed closed-circuit TV in all major grounds, we could have identified [the fans who caused trouble at Portsmouth], had you arrested, hopefully jailed, and certainly banned you from the Bridge. In case any of you are daft enough to consider a repitition [sic] of that behaviour today, remember we have closed-circuit TV here, we are properly stewarded with short-wave radios and we shall not hesitate to take action against anyone who misbehaves.'

TRAINING, NOW AND THEN

'Money changes everything. We used to go to Aberystwyth because it cost us £10 a night to stay in the university digs and you could run on the beach for free and probably pay £20 to the groundsman to use the pitches in the afternoon. Now there's no way the club will go somewhere like Aberystwyth because, for one, there's nowhere could comfortably accommodate the players we've got. Looking back, there's no training facilities good enough for us. No disrespect to Aberystwyth – it was good enough for what we needed at that time. We've moved on to another level and it's all about money.'

1980s defender, 2000s coach Steve Clarke on the changing face of pre-season training

TV DINNER

In 2010/11 Chelsea's income from TV broadcast rights at home and abroad represented 45 per cent of the overall money coming into the club. Following the Premier League's renegotiations with broadcasters in 2012 it is estimated the figure will rise to over 50 per cent.

NAMING RITES

The Stamford Bridge stadium is named after the small bridge on the Fulham Road just outside the main entrance looking east. Its origin is lost in time, but probably derives from the medieval name 'Samfordesbrigge' or Sandy Ford Bridge. The Bridge used to cross a tributary of the Thames called Counter's Creek, which was diverted underground before the present railway line was laid above it in 1863.

43 SECONDS

'It's unbelievable. I just kept running, shot and got very lucky. I've never heard of [Jackie Milburn] but I'm in history – that's not bad.'

Roberto Di Matteo describes his 43-second goal against Middlesbrough in the 1997 FA Cup final at Wembley, which eclipsed Milburn's sluggish 45-second effort in 1955

CAVALIER ATTITUDE

Alec Jackson, Chelsea's famous winger of the early 1930s, known as the 'gay cavalier', scored the equaliser at Maine Road on 16 April 1932 against a Manchester City side that included the latterly famous Matt Busby. The 1–1 draw would prove to be the last of his 77 appearances for the Pensioners. Club officials had been tipped off that the night before the game he had broken protocol by having drinks brought to his hotel room. It was announced that he would never again play for Chelsea, and he was parcelled off to lowly Ashton National of the Lancashire League. A surprise move for such a renowned player – made possible by the £8 a week salary cap applied to all league clubs. The Lancastrians, outside Football League jurisdiction and bankrolled by the National Gas and Oil Engine Company, could pay what they liked and forked out £15 weekly for Jackson's services.

The 5ft 7in Scot previously had a bust-up over pay when French club Nîmes offered him a far bigger whack than he was earning at Stamford Bridge, but it was a disappointing closure to his Chelsea career nonetheless. Jackson sadly died in a road accident in Egypt during the Second World War.

FOR MY NEXT TRICK

Youth product Jimmy Greaves has scored the most hat-tricks in Chelsea's history: 13 between 1957 and 1961.

Portsmouth	(h)	25 Dec 1957	4 goals
Sheffield Wednesday	(a)	15 Feb 1958	3
Wolves	(h)	30 Aug 1958	5
Nottingham Forest	(h)	27 Sep 1958	3
Preston North End	(h)	22 Aug 1959	3
Birmingham City	(h)	16 Sep 1959	3
Preston North End	(a)	19 Dec 1959	5
Wolves	(h)	27 Aug 1960	3
Blackburn Rovers	(h)	7 Sep 1960	3
Manchester City	(h)	19 Nov 1960	3
West Bromwich Albion	(h)	3 Dec 1960	5
Newcastle United	(a)	25 Mar 1961	4
Nottingham Forest	(h)	29 Apr 1961	4
			(his final match)

Bobby Tambling and Kerry Dixon both managed 9 hat-tricks.

'LE OEUF'

How terrace wits described the huge bump on Frank Leboeuf's forehead following a clash with Wimbledon's Robbie Earle in October 1996.

4–0 LOVE

In October 1994, during a break in play for an injury to Paul Furlong, Dennis Wise found himself by the West Stand touchline holding the ball. Ever the entertainer, Dennis found a willing fan in the crowd, Ray Phillips, and embarked on a decent bout of head-tennis until Furlong was fit enough to continue. Chelsea went on to beat Leicester 4–0.

PURPLE PROSE

'[Terry Venables] the calm, complete commander-in-chief as he moved the pins on the map.'

The Guardian, 1965

HARLINGTON

The facilities at Chelsea's 1990s Harlington training ground near Heathrow was a long way from the luxury of purpose-built Cobham. The permanently cold and windswept facilities were owned by Imperial College, whose students enjoyed equal rights of access on certain days. Bemused World Cup winner Marcel Desailly once had his designer clobber removed from a peg and dumped on the bench by a spotty undergraduate while answering an interview question. Another issue was the only telephone on site – a payphone with the money box removed, more reminiscent of a student flat. Chelsea kept a 50p piece in the cavity that could be fed through for credits. During one summer crucial negotiation over a player, Glenn Hoddle had to terminate the call when the pips went – the 50p had fallen onto the floor and the Chelsea boss could not find it amid the mud that had fallen off players' boots.

AS EASY AS AVB

In his brief spell as Chelsea manager André Villas-Boas earned a reputation in press conferences for creating neologisms. Here are some of the nicest:

Criterious (adj.) – *applying principles too readily.*
Efficate (verb) – *to make happen.*
Incentivate (verb) – *to inspire.*
Perspectivate (verb) – *to cause to reflect.*
Solidificate (verb) – *to firm up.*

OUR KEN

Musings from Ken Bates' column in the Chelsea programme:

'Now I know and like these guys [the Sky Sports commentators] but their performance [in coverage of Chelsea's trip to Old Trafford] was a disgrace. It was supposed to be a match commentary, instead they gave a 90-minute eulogy of Manchester United. I suspect that most of the viewers were not Man Utd fans and wanted to watch the match between England's two representatives in the UEFA Champions League quarter-finals. The "Commentator" who [*sic*] also thought that Man Utd had "won in a canter". Try telling that to Frank Leboeuf whose nasty foul by Dwight Yorke went unpunished . . . One thing is for sure, nobody can accuse Chelsea of getting special treatment as a consequence of our commercial alliance with that TV company.'

ONE MATTHEW HARDING

After Chelsea director and multimillionaire 'superfan' Matthew Harding died suddenly on the way back from a match at Bolton in 1996, the club swiftly made arrangements to provide a proper tribute for the ensuing game, the visit of Tottenham. The matchday programme was rejigged and a sign announcing the renaming of the North Stand in his honour prepared. The match became a solemn tribute to the man who had ploughed money into the club, although Chelsea had to turn down an offer from a supporter to fund a band of guardsmen to play 'Abide With Me' prior to kick off. 'It would have become difficult for the players,' said managing director Colin Hutchinson. 'Matthew would not have wanted anything to have interfered with the game.'

TWITTER YE NOT

'I supported Chelsea in 1970. And I still love the way football makes everyone really really angry. For no reason.'

Jeremy Clarkson, 8 May 2012

LETTERS OF NOTE

'Pat Nevin
c/o Chelsea F.C.
Stamford Bridge
Dear Steve,
Thank you very much for taking the time out to write to me. If I do leave I will be very disappointed, the supporters have been great to me, I'll miss them and the "idea" of Chelsea F.C.

I'm sure whatever happens the team is far too good to stay in the 2nd Division. Basically I've said what I wanted to say, thanks for writing, it's good to know people care.
Take care of yourself,
Yours,
Pat.'

**Written by soon-to-depart midfielder Pat Nevin to supporter
Steve Choppin, May 1988**

PLAYER OF THE DECADE: THE 2010s

Didier Drogba 15 Aug 2004 – 19 May 2012
As influential in defence as up front, the Ivory Coast star is arguably the best forward ever to play for Chelsea and the club's fourth highest goalscorer. Even the 100 league goals in 8 seasons, the 9 goals in 9 finals, the two Golden Boots (2006/07

and 2009/10), the 74 caps for his country in his time at Stamford Bridge, barely capture his impact on the club's successes and its perception globally. Tall, athletic, fast and powerful, he was frequently described by opponents as 'unplayable' – as great an honour as any sportsman can earn. Perhaps no one in the game has mastered the solo striker role in a 4-3-3 formation with the same effectiveness. Although he was lethal to goalies from any part of a football field, off it he effectively brought about a ceasefire in his homeland, riven by civil war, and was a great ambassador for Chelsea. Fittingly, he left for Shanghai Shenhua in 2012 having said goodbye with crucial goals against Tottenham, Barcelona, Liverpool and, unforgettably, in the Champions League final.

274 appearances, 157 goals.

THE BATTLE OF ROMA

Leading 4–1 from the home leg, goalless in Roma, Chelsea just needed to keep their nerve and see out time against AS Roma to progress in the 1965 Inter-Cities Fairs Cup. In a tempestuous atmosphere, whipped up by the local media following fights and sendings off at the Bridge, Tommy Docherty directed his men to keep calm and waste time. This they did, to the frustration of a crowd that had seemingly smuggled every kind of projectile into the stadium for the occasion.

The club's medic, Dr Boyne, for example, was hit by a balloon filled with 'recycled' beer – talk about taking the urine!

When teenage Johnny Boyle strolled over to the touchline to take a throw-in he was hit by a full water bottle. He crumpled to the turf unconscious, evidently out for the count. In fact he was making the most of the opportunity. 'I hardly felt it,' he said later, 'but it was a good excuse to use up some time.' He played possum for five minutes while being attended by Harry Medhurst and the unusually fragrant Dr Boyne.

At this point Roma's general secretary took the opportunity to remonstrate with the home fans, appealing for calm and an end to the bombardment, but to his remonstrations they paid no heed. As Boyle took to his feet again, a tomato directed at him instead hit his Italian marker. The furious player turned on his own *tifosi* and shook a fist at them.

Eventually, Chelsea's fluent passing and remarkable resilience began to earn applause from some home sections. But that was merely the lull before the storm as the game ended 0–0, eliminating the hosts.

As the Chelsea coach trundled out of the stadium heavy metal objects rained against the windows, many of which were smashed. The wives were bundled to the floor and players held their kitbags up for protection.

'This was nothing to do with civilisation,' railed Docherty in his later autobiography. 'The fans were just a bunch of animals. The only civilised people around the place were Chelsea.'

PENS

Only two Chelsea keepers have a 100 per cent record when it comes to facing penalties: Willie Foulke (1905/06) saved 10 and Ross Turnbull (2009–12) 4. Jimmy Floyd Hasselbaink (2000–4) has taken the most spot-kicks without missing – 12.

PURPLE PROSE

'To be caught in possession was like standing in the path of a stampede.'

The Times, Chelsea v Leeds FA Cup semi-final, 1967

PSYCHIC

A *Times* writer described the Chelsea side of the mid-1930s as 'a team of talents that doesn't always blend together well.' They remained expensively assembled underachievers . . .

GAME OF THE DECADE: THE 1990s

Chelsea 2–0 Middlesbrough, FA Cup, 17 May 1997
Decades of hurt were blown away after 43 seconds by Italian midfielder Roberto Di Matteo's early goal, and sealed by homegrown Eddie Newton's tap-in. Ruud Gullit became the first overseas (and black) manager ever to lift the trophy.

PLUS 20s

An overlooked record of the 2009/10 Double-winning season was that Didier Drogba (29) and Frank Lampard (22) became the first two Chelsea players to hit 20-plus goals in the same season.

NAME-DROPPED

Announcer on radio set: '. . . West Bromwich Albion 3, Chelsea 5 . . .'
Ben Cutlet (shipwrecked sailor Will Hay): 'Ooh fancy – Chelsea won!'
Island chief: 'What voice in box say?'
Cutlet: 'Something very unusual.'

From the 1936 comedy film *Windbag The Sailor*, starring Will Hay.

NEAR MISSES

Club names and nicknames that were considered along with Chelsea FC and the Pensioners:

Chinamen
Buns
Chelseaites
Stamford Bridge FC
London United FC
Kensington FC

MONEYBAGS

In their sixteenth annual report in July 1921 Chelsea disclosed a gross revenue for the year of £85,482, about £1,000 greater than that of any football club in the country; the next highest was that of Newcastle United.

MOURINHO ON MANAGERS

'I think that a manager today is not what a manager was 20 years ago, or 30 years ago. When sometimes I heard people trying to [compare] managers and saying this one now and the other one 30 years ago, I think it is completely impossible to do it. The only thing we didn't change was the name of our job. There were managers 30 years ago, we are managers now. After that everything changes.'

José Mourinho, 2005

SOFT TOUCH

Chelsea's election to the Football League in 1905/6 came at a price, and clubs 'oop north' made sure the price was paid. At a League meeting in June 1906 Mr Pollitt of Stockport County reminded the Londoners that before being admitted they had promised to pay travelling expenses of £20 to each Northern adversary in their division, and £15 to Midlanders. The resolution was carried and Chelsea forced to cough up.

PENSIONERS AT THE MOVIES

Chelsea players starred in two of the very earliest feature films involving football, as well as England's first ever 'x' certificate in the 1950s.

The Winning Goal (G.B. Samuelson, 1920). Jack Cock plays himself in possibly the first (silent) football film.

The Great Game (Jack Raymond, 1930). Several Chelsea men – and Stamford Bridge – light up this footballer-gets-girl feature. Rex Harrison gets his first credit.

Cosh Boy (Lewis Gilbert, 1953). PT instructor Roy Bentley cameos in this juvenile delinquent cash-in alongside Joan Collins.

CARRY ON DICKIE

Smutty Chelsea players' surnames:

Bush	Feely
Cock	Plum
Dickie	Rodger

REPUTATIONS

'The scene at Chelsea was a remarkable one, and the home club must have reaped a rich harvest, for the whole of the forty turnstiles were in use, and for nearly two hours there was a constant flow of spectators into the ground. When the enclosure was formed [18 months earlier], it was said that no expense had been spared in making the ground the most complete in England, and that condition is now fulfilled. Visitors to Chelsea on Saturday were shown the Club-room which has been provided for the players; it has only lately been finished but its completeness is surprising. There are few better billiard-rooms even in the West End of London. Footballers are undoubtedly men of importance in these days.'

Gloucester Citizen, 1 October 1906

BRING YOUR DINNER

'You, you little ****, when I tell you to do something, and you, you ***ing big ****, when I tell you to do something, do it. And if you come back at me, we'll have a ****ing right sort-out in here. All right? And you can pair up if you like, and you can ****ing pick someone else to help you, and you can bring your ****ing dinner. 'Cos by the time I've finished with you, you'll ****ing need it.'

Manager (and former Chelsea defender) John Sitton's memorable half-time pep-talk during the 1995 documentary *Orient: Club For A Fiver*

AROUND THE GROUNDS

The five teams against whom Chelsea have enjoyed the greatest away success are:

Tottenham Hotspur
Manchester City
West Bromwich Albion
Arsenal
Fulham

The five least fruitful are:

Liverpool
Arsenal
Everton
Newcastle United
Aston Villa

THAT 1994 FA CUP FINAL DEFEAT WE NEVER MENTION

'In '94 I was a player. My big disappointment was that I'd missed the chance of a cup winner's medal. I was a player – I was thinking about me. I didn't think I'd get another chance. Fortunately I was wrong but at that time, after the game, there was no consoling me because I felt I'd had a decent career and I'd got to a cup final and it was my one chance to pick up a winner's medal. And to get hammered in the final 4–0 was doubly disappointing, and to get hammered in the final 4–0 by Man Utd was trebly disappointing. And then you think – at the time I was 31 – "well that's it for me".

I wasn't thinking about the football club; I was purely selfish and thinking about myself.

'[Glenn Hoddle's assistant Graham Rix] said: "You've been here once – you have to resolve to do it again. Remember the feeling and next time you come back, make sure you win it."'

**Steve Clarke, 2005. In 1997 he did indeed pick up his
FA Cup winner's medal**

LETTERS OF NOTE

'It was nauseating at the last home match to observe that the crowd at Chelsea, once considered among the most sporting in the country, descended to singing "Why are we waiting?" because time was taken to put an injured Sheffield United player on a stretcher. Since it is obvious that a man who requires a stretcher is not malingering, this callousness is disgusting.'

B.D. Barnard, Putney, Chelsea programme, September 1967

OVER LAND AND SEA (AND LEICESTER)

Chelsea FC tours 1905–38

1906 – Denmark, Bohemia, Austria, Hungary

13 May	Boldklubben 1893	Copenhagen	6–2 win
14 May	Southampton	Copenhagen	2–1 win
16 May	Deutscher	Prague	4–0 win
17 May	Deutscher	Prague	6–1 win
18 May	Budapesti	Budapest	4–0 win
20 May	Magyar	Budapest	6–0 win
22 May	Ferençvaros	Budapest	3–1 win
24 May	Vienna Cricket	Vienna	3–1 win
26 May	Wiener Ramblers	Vienna	7–0 win
27 May	First Vienna	Vienna	3–0 win

1907 – Netherlands

| 12 May | Haarlemsche | Haarlem | 7–3 win |

1908 – Netherlands

3 May	Everton	Haarlem	4–0 loss

1922 – Denmark

19 May	Copenhagen Select	Copenhagen	1–1 draw
21 May	Copenhagen Select	Copenhagen	2–1 loss

1929 – Argentina, Uruguay, Brazil

25 May	Buenos Aires XI	Buenos Aires	3–2 win
26 May	Provincia	Buenos Aires	4–0 loss
30 May	Argentine Amateur Association	Buenos Aires	1–0 win
2 June	Buenos Aires XI	Buenos Aires	3–2 loss
8 June	San Lorenzo de Almagro	Buenos Aires	2–0 win
9 June	Peñarol	Montevideo	2–1 loss
15 June	Independiente	Buenos Aires	1–1 draw
16 June	Union de Santa Fe	Santa Fe	5–0 loss
16 June	Rosario	Rosario	2–1 loss
20 June	Racing Club	Buenos Aires	1–0 loss
22 June	Estudiantil Porteño	Buenos Aires	3–2 loss
23 June	Wanderers	Montevideo	1–0 win
28 June	Rio de Janeiro XI	Rio de Janeiro	1–1 draw
30 June	Rio de Janeiro XI	Rio de Janeiro	2–1 loss
4 July	Corinthians	São Paulo	4–4 draw
7 July	São Paulo	São Paulo	3–1 loss

1932 – Germany, Netherlands

15 May	Preussen	Berlin	2–0 loss
16 May	Bayern Munich	Munich	2–1 win
21 May	Leipzig XI	Leipzig	7–3 win
22 May	Stuttgarter Kickers	Stuttgart	2–0 win
26 May	Rotterdam XI	Rotterdam	2–1 win

1934 – Netherlands

12 May	Holland Select	Amsterdam	3–2 win

1936 – Netherlands, Sweden, Poland

9 May	Blauw-Wit	Amsterdam	3–2 win
13 May	AIK	Stockholm	6–0 win

19 May	Sweden XI	Gothenburg	4–0 win
23 May	· Poland XI	Warsaw	2–0 win
24 May	Wisla Krakow	Krakow	1–0 loss

1937 – Austria, Yugoslavia, France

17 May	Vienna	Vienna	3–0 loss
19 May	Steiermark	Graz	2–4 loss
24 May	Belgrade	Belgrade	1–6 loss
27 May	Gradjanski	Zagreb	1–0 win
30 May	Olympique Marseille	Paris	1–1 draw
3 Jun	Austria Vienna	Paris	2–0 win
6 Jun	Bologna	Paris	4–1 loss

1938 – Denmark

16 May	Staevnet	Copenhagen	3–1 win
18 May	Staevnet	Copenhagen	4–1 win
20 May	Denmark XI	Copenhagen	2–0 win

CLUB AND COUNTRY

Including wartime 'guests', five England managers have previously played for Chelsea: Sir Walter Winterbottom, Joe Mercer, Ron Greenwood, Terry Venables and Glenn Hoddle.

LONDON UNITED

The first time Chelsea players were involved in a cup competition in Europe, they weren't even playing for Chelsea, though they were playing a home game at Stamford Bridge.

The tournament was the Inter-Cities Fairs Cup, devised the same season, 1955, as the European Champions Clubs' Cup (to give the senior trophy its formal title). Chelsea should have entered the inaugural European Cup but were hardlined out of doing so by the FA's Alan Hardaker.

The Fairs Cup was not a UEFA-run tournament and was open to teams from any city that had held a trade fair with some, like London, entering a combined XI.

Bizarrely, Chelsea chairman Joe Mears was made manager of the London XI, which included several players familiar to him at the Bridge: Ken Armstrong, Derek Saunders, Stan Wicks, Jimmy Greaves, Peter Sillett, Jim Lewis and Brian Nicholas. It had an unwieldy format, with a group stage alone that ranged over two years beginning in June 1955 and ending in March 1957.

Greaves scored in the October 1957 semi-final win over Lausanne Sports of Switzerland to record a 3–2 aggregate win for the white-shirted Londoners.

The two-legged final against Barcelona was played the following spring, with Lewis figuring in both legs and Greaves netting in the first, a 2–2 draw at Stamford Bridge. Without Greaves the capital's finest were beaten 6–0 at Camp Nou.

1955–8 Inter-Cities Fairs Cup – matches involving London XI

Group D

Sat 4 Jun 1955	Basle XI 0–5 London XI
Wed 26 Oct 1955	London XI 3–2 Frankfurt XI
Fri 4 May 1956	London XI 1–0 Basle XI
Wed 27 Mar 1957	Frankfurt XI 1–0 London XI

Semi-final

Mon 16 Sep 1957	Lausanne Sports 2–1 London XI
Wed 23 Oct 1957	London XI 2–0 Lausanne Sports (at Highbury)

Final

Wed 5 Mar 1958	London XI 2–2 Barcelona
Thu 1 May 1958	Barcelona 6–0 London XI

STAMFORD BLAZE

A former soldier, Mr Truro, walked through and knelt down in a bed of fire at Stamford Bridge during a demonstration of a flame-resistant treatment he had invented in 1920. His khaki uniform remained unsinged but sadly we have no record of whether his product was commercially successful or his investment went up in smoke.

MOST HOME WINS IN A SEASON

1906/07	18 from 19 in Division 2	(95%)
1910/11	19 from 19 in Division 2	(100%)
1929/30	17 from 21 in Division 2	(81%)
1962/63	15 from 21 in Division 2	(71%)
1964/65	15 from 21 in Division 1	(71%)
2005/06	18 from 19 in Premier League	(95%)

CROSSBAR

In 1967 a new crossbar cost £49. We know this because supporters invaded the pitch after a friendly Chelsea played against the GB Olympic XI on Monday 4 September, and some youngsters hung on a bar and snapped it. Half-price admission for juveniles was withdrawn by the club in cruel retribution.

INTO THE BREACH

Fans always love the moment an outfield player has to deputise for an absent goalkeeper – less frequent since the number of subs was increased. Here are some who have performed such temporary heroics for Chelsea:

David Webb
Ron Tindall
Bert Murray
Bill Garner
Tommy Langley
David Speedie
John Coady
Vinnie Jones
Glen Johnson
John Terry

REPUTATIONS

'Then there is the most numerous set in Chelsea, that lives round by Lots Road, away towards Fulham. It consists of people who are more likely to have heard of Chelsea Football Club than Augustus John.'

John Betjeman, 'London's Bohemia' article,
***Picture Post*, 5 November 1938**

BIT LATE NOW

'Everyone who knows the laws of the game knows I should have done things differently, but that's the life of a referee.'
Admission, three years on, by 2009 Champions League semi-final referee Tom Henning Ovrebo, who denied at least four clear penalty claims by the Blues against Barcelona

ONE IN FIVE

By winning the UEFA Champions League the Blues became just the fifth English club to lift the prestigious trophy (formerly the European Cup), the others being Liverpool, Manchester United, Nottingham Forest and Aston Villa.

FIRST . . .

Manager – John Tait 'Jackie' Robertson (player-manager).

Captain – Willie Foulke.

Match – home to Liverpool, friendly, 4 September 1905 (won 4–0).

Official match – away to Stockport County, Division Two, 1 September 1905 (lost 1–0).

Official win – away to Blackpool, Division Two, 9 September 1905 (won 1–0).

Official goalscorer – John Tait Robertson, away to Blackpool, Second Division, 9 September 1905 (won 1–0).

Opponent own goal – v. Gainsborough Trinity, 16 December 1905 (won 2–0).

Penalty saved – Willie Foulke from Schofield of Stockport County, Edgeley Park, 2 September 1905.

Penalty scored – Bob McRoberts, against Barnsley at the Bridge, 4 November 1905.

60,000+ crowd – Chelsea 1–1 Manchester United, 13 April 1906 (attendance: 67,000).

Sending off – Jimmy Windridge, away to Nottingham Forest (0–0), 5 March 1910 (momentary disgrace (retaliation)).

First FA Cup qualifying round match – home to First Grenadier Guards, first qualifying round, 7 October 1905 (won 6–1).

FA Cup match – v. Lincoln City, first round, 12 January 1907 (drew 2–2).

London derby – Clapton Orient 0–3 Chelsea, Millfields Road, 11 November 1905.

Top-flight London derby – Chelsea 2–1 Arsenal, Stamford Bridge, 9 November 1907.

Overseas player – Nils Middelboe, debut 15 November 1913.

FA Cup final – v. Sheffield United, Old Trafford, 24 April 1915.

Silverware – 1919 Victory Cup 3–0 v Fulham at Highbury.

80,000+ crowd – Chelsea 1–1 Arsenal, 12 October 1935.

Black player signed – Fred Hanley, from Skelmersdale, 1938.

League Cup match – v. Millwall, first round, 10 October 1960 (won 7–1).

League Cup final victory – 1965, won 3–2 on aggregate over Leciester City.

Substitute – John Boyle for George Graham, v. Fulham, 28 August 1965.

Substitute for a goalkeeper – Bill Garner for Peter Bonetti, v. Luton, Division Two, 16 April 1976 (1–1 at the time, ended 2–2).

FA Cup final victory – 1970.

UEFA Cup Winners' Cup victory – 1971.

European match – v. BK Frem, Fairs Cup, 30 September 1958 (won 3–1).

UEFA Cup Winners' Cup match – v. Aris Salonika, first round, 16 September 1970 (drew 1–1).

UEFA Champions League qualifying match – v. Skonto Riga, third qualifying round, 11 August 1999 (won 3–0).

UEFA Champions League match – v. AC Milan, first group stage, 15 September 1999 (drew 0–0).

FA Cup victory at the New Wembley Stadium – v. Manchester United, FA Cup Final, 19 May 2007 (won 1–0 aet).

UEFA Cup Winners' Cup and League Cup Double – 1998.

Premier League and League Cup Double – 2005.

FA Cup and League Cup Double – 2007.

League and FA Cup Double – v. Portsmouth FC, FA Cup final, 15 May 2010 (won 1–0) and winning the Premier League with 86 points.

UEFA Champions League and FA Cup Double – 2012.

100 League Goals in a season – 2009/10 Premier League season.

THE THREE Cs

'Chelsea FC, Courage bitter and Crumpet' – according to Sid Abbot (Sid James) of 1970s sitcom, *Bless This House*.

CELERY SORTS

Adapted from an old parlour ditty or rugby song, and reputedly first heard at Oxford United away on August bank holiday 1986, the 'celery song' is one of the Chelsea fans' most distinctive and quirky terrace anthems.

The words 'Celeree . . . celeree! If she don't come I'll tickle her bum with a lump of celery! Celeree . . .' are accompanied by the celebratory tossing of sprigs of the vegetable back and forth. Several bunches appeared among memorials to Matthew Harding left at Stamford Bridge following his tragic death in 1996, and Cesc Fabregas complained of celery flak during the 2007 League Cup final.

Meanwhile Manchester United winger Ryan Giggs chuckled about the practice in his autobiography, and it amused Christopher Davies during Chelsea's 1–0 FA Cup semi-final win over Fulham in 2002: 'The Chelsea fans . . . threw pieces of celery at Fulham chairman Mohamed Fayed in the directors' box before the match. Two muscular security men stood behind Fayed to protect him from the flying food. It is a Chelsea tradition to wave sticks of celery and chant the name of the vegetable, which is acceptable if a little unusual. However, a tossed salad is not so appetising when it arrives in such a manner.'

Gloomily, this contravenes the Football Act 1991, and five Chelsea supporters were bound over to keep the peace following that Fulham match (no, that's not 'keep the peas').

VOTING WITH THE WALLET

Fernando Torres (from Liverpool to Chelsea) and Andy Carroll (from Newcastle to Liverpool) were the big stories of the January 2011 transfer window. In a shirt sales report at the close of the season, the name of the Blues' new boy outstripped that of the Merseysiders' replacement no. 9 by 250 to 1.

7-UP

In unofficial matches, has any Chelsea player bettered Tommy Lawton's haul of all seven in the Pensioners' 7–1 thrashing of Young Boys at the Wankdorf Stadium, Bern, Switzerland, in 1946? One local paper described how five minutes from the end Lawton 'calmly, but with a cannonball shot, marked the seventh, to endless applause.'

COME ON DOWN!

The fortunate recipient of first prize in the 'Lucky Programme Draw' for Micky Droy's Testimonial in May 1983 (50p a ticket, or five for £2) became the proud owner of:

A BRAND NEW FORD FIESTA
Plus: Sun Roof
Stereo Cassette
Fog Lamps
Road Fund Licence
Numberplates

LETTERS OF NOTE

'We believe both Leeds cup final goals should have been disallowed – the first because Jack Charlton impeded goalkeeper Peter Bonetti and the second because Peter Lorimer obstructed Chelsea defender John Dempsey to allow Mick Jones his scoring shot.'

'23 Chelsea fans,' *Daily Mirror,* **15 April 1970**

BOOTY

In 1908, at a sports day inside Millwall FC's stadium, a long-kicking contest was won by the hosts' goalie, John 'Tiny' Joyce, who managed 254ft. Chelsea's Bob 'Pom Pom' Whiting was second with 251ft 5in.

MINI LEAP FOR MANKIND

Eccentric Duncan McKenzie was with Chelsea for barely half of the 1978/79 season but almost attained cult hero status. Not only had he appeared in the official programme (before arriving at Stamford Bridge) several times 'introducing' us supporters to a new lager beer from Belgium, but his party pieces included the ability to jump over a Mini from a standing start. Every teenage boy's dream, obviously.

SOUTHERN PREJUDICE

Chelsea originally kept their options open and applied for admission to the Football League and the Southern League in spring 1905. However, when the Southern heard of Chelsea's application to their rival they jealously rejected the new club – perhaps under pressure from their existing London clubs Fulham and Tottenham. Chelsea ended up being admitted to the Football League Division Two, starting in 1905/06.

LETTERS OF NOTE

'Dear Mr Birrell,

May I take this opportunity of letting you know how much I and many thousands of others appreciate the "new look programme."

There is one suggestion I would like to make. All followers of football have read much about "players' wages" in the Press recently and this subject is still being discussed. But why cannot we, the supporters of Chelsea, have an opportunity of contributing to a player's benefit? The maximum figure which a club is allowed to pay is, I believe, £650 for each period of five years. But is there anything to stop supporters, as distinct from their club, organising a collection for a particular player at one particular game and the sum being presented to the player quite independently? I have heard of Third Division clubs doing this.

Would not this be a grand way of letting us express our appreciation of a player? I am certain volunteers could be found to help organise such an undertaking which would, I imagine, have to be organised without any assistance from the parent club.

Something on these lines was organised for Tommy Walker. Surely players like Dicky Spence, Albert Tennant and Dicky Foss, who have given the club such grand service, deserve all we can do for them?

I hope perhaps you will find time to answer this letter sometime, either personally or through the medium of your programme.'

C.S. Cheshire, Chelsea programme, 2 April 1949

Scott Cheshire, born 1926, was for many years the great unofficial historian of Chelsea FC.

SOME MANAGERS OF THE MONTH

December 1969	Dave Sexton
August 1976	Eddie McCreadie
October 1980	Geoff Hurst
December 1985	John Hollins
September 2003	Claudio Ranieri
March 2004	Claudio Ranieri

November 2004	José Mourinho
January 2005	José Mourinho
March 2007	José Mourinho
April 2008	Avram Grant
November 2009	Carlo Ancelotti
August 2010	Carlo Ancelotti
March 2011	Carlo Ancelotti
April 2011	Carlo Ancelotti

WINDOW OF OPPORTUNITY

Things were going badly wrong towards the close of the 1909/10 season. After a 5–2 defeat at bottom side Bolton on 12 February, injury-ravaged Chelsea were fighting against relegation and responded by splashing the then remarkable sum of £3,300 on several panic buys, including English McConnell and Bob Whittingham. To the delight of opponents the spree failed, with some new players joining the sick list and relegation following in April. There was a further-reaching impact though: registration problems connected to the transfers led the FA to rule that future player transfers would have to be cleared by the fourth Thursday of March at 3 p.m. each season. Chelsea had indirectly created the 'transfer deadline', forerunner of today's 'transfer window'.

HURRY UP HAROLD

There is also a Stamford Bridge on the River Derwent in Yorkshire – the site of Harold Godwinson's victory over Viking invaders led by King Harald Hardrada of Norway and the English king's brother Tostig Godwinson on 25 September 1066. Just a fortnight later Harold met his fate at the battle of Hastings in Sussex. In 1905 Chelsea would receive letters post-marked Yorkshire with the words 'Not this Stamford Bridge, try London' written on them – this was the reason Stamford Bridge FC was rejected as a possible name for the new team.

WRITTEN IN THE STARS

Each time a European Cup/Champions League final has been staged in Munich a new name has been inscribed on the trophy: Nottingham Forest in 1979, Marseille in 1993, Borussia Dortmund in 1997 and Chelsea in 2012.

AMATEUR MASTERCHEF

Iconic brute defender Mickey Droy was awarded a Testimonial match for November 1983 to be played against Arsenal. The mountainous centre-half asked the then Stamford Bridge catering manager Leon Lenik to cut a deal on food. Lenik, a lifelong Blues fan, was agreeable, but only in return for a role in the game, and before kick-off was putting on kit to be a substitute along with the regular players.

They approved of his culinary skills, but his footballing qualities were an unknown quantity. As it turned out the friendly was surprisingly feisty and recent signing Charlie Nicholas opened the scoring for the north Londoners.

During the interval, coach John Hollins turned to Alan Hudson and told him that Lenik would be his replacement after ten minutes. Hudson gave the caterer a wink and invited him to take his place right away instead.

There was some humour in the stands when the stadium announcer explained Lenik's pedigree, but his first few touches revealed an accomplished footballer.

The restaurateur helped Chelsea overturn the scoreline and win 2–1, with Gunners' boss Terry Neill supposedly railing at his side that a chef could almost cook up a goal. That backline, incidentally, included Tony Adams for the first time.

Lenik's shirt was signed by all and retained as a souvenir. Meanwhile the catering manager revealed that as youngster he had impressed enough to attend England schoolboy trials, and been asked to sign as an apprentice professional! In fact Lenik began to train regularly with the team.

Eventually, though, he moved on to take up a similar role at Brentford, and on 14 May 1984 Eddie Lyons' Testimonial was held at Griffin Park against Chelsea, with Lenik on as substitute once more.

However this time his cameo was less laudable: when Kerry Dixon called, 'Leon, give me the ball!' familiarity led to contempt as Lenik passed to his former team-mate. And so one of Dixon's five goals that night came from the catering manager's assist.

THE WHOLE TRUTH, NOTHING BUT THE TRUTH

Prosecutor in John Terry trial: 'You are the current European Champions, and John Terry is a Chelsea legend?'
Chelsea chairman Bruce Buck: 'Yes.'

TYPICAL CHELSEA SIGNING

Joe Payne arrived from Luton Town in 1938 with the unique monicker 'Ten goal'. His tally for the Hatters remains the most scored in a league game, but he was a utility player before converting to centre forward for the fateful encounter with Bristol Rovers. Prior to kick-off the club's chairman had advised Joe, 'Don't stop when you get three goals will you – just go on and get another three.' 'Right,' thought Payne, 'I'll get another three to make sure.' Two years later he signed for Chelsea, and scored many opportunist goals – 22 in 47 appearances before war came again.

GLAMOUR CLUB

There are more than 100 items of popular music with 'Chelsea' in the title, ranging from Joni Mitchell's 'Chelsea Morning' to The Fratellis' 'Chelsea Dagger'. Only Liverpool comes remotely close to pricking the musical muse. There are just over a dozen titles including the word 'Arsenal' and little more that include 'Manchester'. And people just don't sing seem to want sing about Tottenham at all.

HOME CROWD MILESTONES

Chelsea are one of just nine clubs to have recorded the highest attendance in the country.

1906/07	Highest average home attendance in Division Two (18,425).
1907/08	First British club to exceed 30,000 average home attendance (32,895).
1910/11	Highest average home attendance in Division Two (23,850).
1911/12	First Division Two club to record highest average home attendance in the country (26,400).
1912/13	Highest average home attendance in Britain (32,100).
1913/14	Set new UK record for average home attendance of 37,900.
1919/20	First British club to exceed 40,000 average home attendance (42,860).
1921/22	Highest average home attendance in the country (37,160).
1923/24	Highest average home attendance in the UK (30,710).
1925/26	As a Division Two club, record highest average home attendance in the country (32,355). Biggest crowd in division (49,707 v Blackpool).
1928/29	As a Division Two club, record highest average home attendance in the UK (28,017). Biggest crowd in division (48,775 v Middlesbrough).
1928/29	As a Division Two club, record highest average home attendance in Britain (27,799).
1929/30	Biggest crowd in Division Two (53,819 v Blackpool).
1930/31	Biggest crowd in Division One (74,667 v Arsenal).
1931/32	Biggest crowd in Division One (64,427 v Arsenal).
1932/33	Biggest crowd in Division One (72,260 v Arsenal).
1935/36	Biggest crowd in Division One – and club's history (82,905 v Arsenal).
1937/38	Biggest crowd in Division One (75,952 v Arsenal).
1946/47	Biggest crowd in Division One (67,935 v Stoke).
1952/53	Biggest crowd in Division One (72,614 v Arsenal).
1954/55	Record highest average home attendance in the country, and biggest in club's history (48,260).

1959/60   Biggest crowd in Division One (67,819 v Tottenham).
1962/63   Biggest crowd in Division Two (66,199 v Stoke).
1976/77   Biggest crowd in Division Two (55,003 v Fulham).
2005/06   Highest average home attendance of all-seater stadium (41,902).
2012/13   The 40 millionth top-flight spectator will pass through the Stamford Bridge turnstiles.

SUE MOTT IT BE

'Both communism and Chelsea signed up to the notion of democracy, but to the outside eye, one was, and one can look like, dictatorship in action. The Politburo used the KGB to achieve their ends. They ruled through fear. Chelsea are merely using banknotes, a chain of banknotes that could stretch from London to Siberia, to attain their necessary dominance. They are not an evil empire, merely avaricious. But if their avarice is satisfied, evil will befall the sport . . . As long as Chelsea's owner is alive, well and wealthy, football has got a big problem.'

Sue Mott, *Daily Telegraph*, June 2005

GAME OF THE DECADE: THE 2000s

Bolton 0–2 Chelsea, Premier League, 30 April 2005
Chelsea were at last crowned champions again after a 50-year wait, and exactly when manager José Mourinho had predicted, Frank Lampard fittingly netting both goals at the Reebok Stadium.

SPECIAL ONE MARK ONE

'Chelsea are the greatest club I've known. The people here have taken it on the chin for 50 years and always come up smiling. That takes some doing.'

Chelsea manager Ted Drake, in his speech after winning
the club's first league title in 1955

THE FIRST EUROPEAN CUP?

1954/55 league champions Chelsea were prevented by the Little Englanders of the Football League from participating in the inaugural 1955/56 European Cup, despite attending all the planning meetings. However, the Pensioners did take part in an early version of the elite competition, the Tournoi International de l'Expo Universelle de Paris, in 1937. First contested in 1931 (with Wolves as England's representative) the May/June tournament pitted Chelsea against top clubs from France, Germany, Italy, Czechoslovakia, Hungary and Austria.

Chelsea progressed to the final where they lost 4–1 to Italian champions Bologna – whose president, Renato dall'Ara instantly declared the triumph 'a victory for Fascism.'

Quarter-finals (30 May)
FK Austria Wien 2–0 VfB Leipzig (played at Le Havre)
SK Slavia Prague 2–1 Phöbus FC (Strasbourg)
Chelsea FC 1–1 Olympique de Marseille (Antibes)
    Chelsea won on lots drawn.
AGC Bologna 4–1 FC Sochaux-Montbéliard (Paris)

Semi-finals (3 Jun)
Chelsea FC 2–0 FK Austria Wien (Paris)
AGC Bologna 2–0 SK Slavia Prague (Lille)

Third Place play-off (5 Jun)
SK Slavia Prague 3–0 FK Austria Wien (Saint-Ouen)

Tournoi Final (6 Jun)
AGC Bologna 4–1 Chelsea FC (Paris)

OPENING THE ACCOUNT

Chelsea's first goal in official competition was scored, fittingly, by player-manager John Tait 'Jackie' Robertson in a 1–0 win at Blackpool's Bloomfield Road on 9 September 1905.

ANOTHER CHELSEA

'Chelsea [porcelain] has the distinction of being perhaps the most successful of English factories in copying the products of Continental establishments.'

Apollo, A Journal of the Arts, **1948**

'Chelsea are a Continental team playing football in England.'

Colin Hutchinson, Chelsea FC managing director, 2000

WHITING WRONGS

Bob Whiting played more than 50 games for the Pensioners between April 1906 and December 1907, his powerful upfield kicks earning him the nickname 'Pom-Pom' – after British anti-aircraft cannon. A few months after war came in 1914 he joined the Footballers' Battalion and served in France until sent home with scabies in 1916. However, during a lengthy spell away from the front in a military hospital, he went absent without leave. Months later he was arrested and found guilty of desertion – a charge for which some soldiers had faced the firing squad. However, on the very same day as the verdict there was another delivery: his wife Nellie gave birth to their third son, Joseph (conceived the week Pom-Pom had gone AWOL).

To the family's relief Whiting was actually sentenced to imprisonment. This was short-lived, though, as he was suddenly ordered back to France as fodder for the Ypres Offensive. Without seeing his wife or two-month-old child again, Pom-Pom was killed by a shell on 28 April 1917, his body never identified. Back home, cruel stories emerged that he had actually been shot in the back as a coward. His distraught widow Nellie was even forced to publish a letter of commendation from his commanding officer in local newspapers to clear his name. Pom-Pom is one of four known Chelsea-related fatalities of the First World War, and in 2010 was among those soldiers commemorated in a stained-glass window display at Westminster Abbey.

GAME OF MARPLES

The Conservative MP for Wallasey (1945–74) Ernest Marples was a keep fit fanatic who believed in fasting for a fortnight each year, during which time his only fluid intake (unusually for a Westminster habitué) would be water. In the 1950s he would rise at 5 a.m. in his Victoria home, cycle a while, then train with the Chelsea players at Stamford Bridge before fulfilling his parliamentary duties.

WINNING STREAKS

Chelsea's longest league victory sequences are as follows:

13	home	26 Nov 1910 – 22 Apr 1911
11	away	5 Apr 2008 – 6 Dec 2008
11	both	25 Apr 2009 – 20 Sep 2009

In any competition, Chelsea's longest victory sequences are as follows:

12	home	17 Apr 2009 – 21 Nov 2009
8	away	25 Feb 2007 – 18 Apr 2007
9	both	7 Aug 2005 – 24 Sep 2005

FINE WINE

Dickie Spence played his final game for the Blues against Bolton at home on 13 September 1947. He was 39 years and 57 days old at the time – the oldest to don the famous royal blue.

PLAYING UP

'I always remember we did a tour of Canada and North America and on the plane were Lord Chelsea, now Earl Cadogan, and I think Brian (Mears) was with us, and we were up the back end of the plane, helping the stewardess out the back; not cleaning the plates up – just chatting them up. Another stewardess came and said, "There's trouble with the players. One player in the party, he's being a bit boisterous and he won't shut up."

'So the directors said to me, "You'd better sort it out John, see who it is." 'So I went back, and guess who it was? Tommy Docherty!'

Former club secretary John Battersby, 2005

TWITTER YE NOT

'Wow!!!! Not a bad bad year for Chelsea!!!! What a double!!! Nice last touch for Chelsea DDA Drogba!!!!'

Golfer Justin Rose, 19 May 2012

REPUTATIONS

'I think especially here at Stamford Bridge is a certain style of supporter. For example in Lisbon, we have Benfican supporters, and I used to say Sporting supporters are supporters with a tie and a jacket, and Benfican supporters are the supporters with a loud voice and a t-shirt and a scarf.

'But I think [Chelsea fans] are not the crazy fanatic supporter who push the team to the victory. But the feeling is there and you go on the street and they are polite people and very nice people but always showing the happiness and the relation with the team and "We have to win tomorrow".'

José Mourinho, 2005

SUSPENSE

Centre forward Bob Turnbull was suspended for two months by the FA from November 1926 following an incident in a match at South Shields the month before. It is the longest ban ever imposed on a Chelsea player, matched in January 1931 by Hughie Gallacher, who was punished for using 'filthy' language at a referee.

TWITTER YE NOT

'If #Chelsea wouldn't be my team I would hate them. But they are so I love them. Yeeeeeeeeeeeeees.'

Former player and manager Ruud Gullit, after Chelsea knocked Barcelona out of the 2012 Champions League

THE ROAD TO MUNICH (2)

The Round of 16 tie pitted Chelsea against a Napoli with the 'three tenors' in attack: Lavezzi, Cavani and Hamsik. The dangerous Neapolitans had already edged out Man City in Group A as runners-up to Bayern Munich and set about the uncoordinated Londoners with relish. They were already 3–1 up when Ashley Cole, with typical intuition and athleticism, hooked a possible fourth off the line. We can never tell how vital Cole's clearance was, but it was not enough to save his manager's job; up stepped Italian assistant Roberto Di Matteo on a temporary basis, and the turnaround was as remarkable as it was instant.

It began with the second leg at home to Napoli, Ramires fashioning a breakthrough goal for Drogba inside the opening half hour. Even when pegged back to 2–1 by the Neapolitans the relentless Blues triumphed through a Lampard penalty and a volley from Ivanovic, who had no cause to be lurking inside the opposition box. It was a thrilling 5–4 aggregate win that resuscitated the Blues' season. At the same stage AC Milan left Arsenal sleeping with the fishes, making Chelsea London's – and England's – sole remaining diners at Europe's top table.

DE-LISTED

A myth has persisted about the Darbourne and Darke-designed East Stand, completed in the 1970s, and still towering over the Stamford Bridge pitch like a rusty, cloaked spectre. Although it has been praised in the architecture world it has never, despite suggestions to the contrary, been one of English Heritage's Listed Buildings.

EARLY BEEB

One of the earliest football commentaries on radio came live from Stamford Bridge on 26 March 1927, just a few months after the BBC had been handed its royal charter. The match was the FA Cup semi-final between Southampton and Arsenal, the commentators George Allison and D. McCulloch.

ACTORS IN TRAINING

Richard Attenborough toughened himself up for the role of Pinkie in the film *Brighton Rock* by training with Chelsea's Tommy Lawton and co. in 1947, beginning the actor's long love affair with the club.

A PREMIER FIRST

Chelsea's first goal of the Premier League era was netted by striker Mick Harford on his debut, a 1–1 draw with Oldham Athletic, on 15 August 1992.

MATS AND DOGS

That Stamford Bridge hosted greyhound racing on a cinder track around the pitch between 1932 and 1968 is well known. What is less so is that in 1927 Joe Mears senior, attempted to stage dog races at the stadium he owned – on carpet. 'We are going to have a carpeted track,' he said, 'because dogs run much better on that than on cinder track. It will be easier for them and will probably produce faster running. It will be a special kind of carpeting that can be laid down or taken up in a few hours.' And we wonder why the club was then a laughing stock . . .

TWITTER YE NOT

'The @chelseafc bus is going past my house. Wish the boys would stop off for tea. Have cake ready!'

TV chef Nigella Lawson, watching the victory parade,
20 May 2012

NAME-DROPPED

In a 1955 *Daily Express* article on '101 Things That A Man Might Expect From His Future Wife', alongside tongue-in-cheek advice such as 'Keep quiet about the sweat of preparing a five-course dinner. Coo over the coffee he made afterwards', is the following: 'You are expected to *enjoy* listening to Chelsea v. Arsenal on the radio.'

TYPICAL CHELSEA SIGNING

Edgar Kail is a legend of south London football. An England amateur international, he scored 400 goals for Dulwich Hamlet between 1919 and 1933, helping the club attracted crowds of 15,000. The approach to their ground is called Edgar Kail Way. In 2003, when Southwark Council requested nominations for local heroes to receive commemorative plaques, they received more for Kail than for William Shakespeare. Yet in March 1930 newspapers confirmed that Kail's registration had been snapped up by soon-to-be-promoted Chelsea. For whatever reason, the brilliant non-league footballer never played for the Pensioners' first team, though, his career ending three years later at Dulwich. Perhaps Chelsea's signing of one of the all-time great strikers, Hughie Gallacher, that summer had something to do with it.

WEMBLEY WAIVED

Chelsea and Arsenal fought a torrid battle in the 1946/7 FA Cup, and were inseparable after a first replay. Such was the interest in the local derby between the third (the Pensioners) and fifth (the

Gunners) best-supported clubs in the country that Chelsea proposed the Empire Stadium, Wembley, as the stadium to stage the second replay. The FA rejected the idea and the third round tie was played at White Hart Lane. Chelsea were eventually victorious with two goals from star striker Tommy Lawton.

Chelsea 1–1 Arsenal	Stamford Bridge	Att: 70,257
Arsenal 1–1 Chelsea	Highbury	Att: 53,350 (1st replay)
Arsenal 0–2 Chelsea	White Hart Lane	Att: 59,590 (2nd replay)

IT'LL NEVER CATCH ON

In 1968 M. Forey of Sullivan Court, Fulham, proposed supporters chorus the following rousing tribute to 'wizard of the dribble' Charlie Cooke, to the tune of 'Charlie Is My Darling':

Charlie is my darling, my darling, my darling
Charlie is my darling, the Chelsea Cavalier;

When he is in possession, then opponents need to fear,
He'll jink and weave, defenders leave
A-toiling in the rear;

Oh! His ball control is magic, he is without a peer,
So take a look at Charlie Cooke,
The Chelsea Cavalier.

Charlie is my darling, my darling, my darling
Charlie is my darling, the Chelsea Cavalier;

His swerves and sways deserve the praise, an artist to revere,
His conjured tricks, and crafty flicks,
Are things that must endear;

Oh! Defenders are uneasy, they have good cause to fear,
When first they look at Charlie Cooke,
The Chelsea Cavalier.

TWITTER YE NOT

'Every English man should be proud of Chelsea! Even Arsenal and Spurs fans!'

Arsenal midfielder Jack Wilshere reacts to Chelsea's Champions League triumph

LETTERS OF NOTE

'Sir, Peter Osgood, I read in your Sports columns, has been taken off the transfer list: "He was put up for sale . . . two weeks ago . . . at £250,000."

I do not suppose slaves sold by auction a century or so ago fetched anything like that price. In the one case you bought the exclusive use of a man's physical labour; in the other, you are buying the exclusive use of a man's skill in kicking a round leather object between two vertical lengths of timber. Otherwise, is there any essential difference between the two transactions?'

Written by Stelio Hourmouzios, Savile Club, London, to
***The Times*, 1971**

ROYAL CHELSEA

The first rulers of any country to watch Chelsea at Stamford Bridge hailed from Swaziland, a small British High Commission territory in southern Africa. Led by Prince Malunga Ka Mbandeni (son of the widowed Queen Regent, Nabotsibeni), the five chiefs sat in the grandstand on Saturday 23 November 1907 to enjoy a First Division match at Stamford Bridge against Bristol City, which Chelsea won 4–1. The real business of these 'dusky rulers' (as the *Daily Express* dubbed them) was to gather support from the British government in opposition to a portion of their land being annexed by South Africa, which was granted.

THE ROMAN EFFECT

'I don't know you know, maybe a lot of people say, "When Mourinho arrived Abramovich was there, and when the [previous managers] arrived Abramovich was not there." Maybe some can think that way and that was the risk that I know I was going to have in a club like Chelsea. Because you come, you change things, you work a lot, you do – in my opinion – very good work, and in the end of the day some people can still think that with Abramovich behind him it, it's easy. I don't say it's easy, I say it is easier.'

José Mourinho, 2005

MY WORD!

'Remember those jokes about the Pensioners? No more of those now. Watch those boys go! The first one comes from Parsons' head. And doesn't that head get a ruffling by his jubilant team-mates. . . . A penalty goal by Sillett. A third goal by Parsons soon after, and it's all over. Chelsea, for the first time in their career, are top of the league . . . Well done Chelsea.'

British Pathé's Bob Danvers-Walker describing the win over Sheffield Wednesday as Chelsea won their first ever title in 1955

BELIEF IN HOD

'The club stepped up when they brought Glenn [Hoddle] in [in 1994]. They brought a manager in who'd been a successful player. He was high profile, good with the media – the media loved him. He'd had experience abroad, he brought in fresh ideas, new training, a different way of playing, a lot of ball-oriented training – making the team play football. And around that time, Matthew [Harding] was trying to force his way into the picture. I think he wanted to take over the club. He wanted the chairman out. I'll never criticise Ken Bates because for me he was fantastic. From day one I always got on with Ken. But what Matthew did was stir him into action. He gave him a little push and Ken suddenly realised he had a challenge to keep his position as chairman. He realised the fans were looking at Matthew and saying, "If he can put in money, why can't you put in money?" And suddenly the money was coming in and we were signing better players – maybe not in the transfer fees but the wages were going up. And Glenn and Matthew, the combination . . . Matthew decided he would become friendly with Glenn. Ken saw it coming and, not a daft man, he responded to the challenge and put more money in, and as a result the club improved. Since then, we've always been working towards reaching the top.'

Steve Clarke, 2005, on the Hoddle-driven Chelsea revolution

FOREIGN LEGION

On Boxing Day 1999 Chelsea became the first English club to field a starting XI comprised entirely of overseas players. They won 2–1 at Southampton.

1   Ed de Goey, Netherlands
2.   Dan Petrescu, Romania (replaced by 20. Jody Morris, England)
3.   Celestine Babayaro, Nigeria
5.   Frank Leboeuf, France
7.   Didier Deschamps, France
8.   Gus Poyet, Uruguay
16.   Roberto Di Matteo, Italy
17.   Albert Ferrer, Spain
18.   Gabriele Ambrosetti, Italy (replaced by 34. Jon Harley, England)
19.   Tore Andre Flo, Norway
30.   Emerson Thome, Brazil

Goalscorers – Flo (2)

Unused substitutes – 22. Mark Nicholls, England; 23. Carlo Cudicini, Italy; 26. John Terry, England.

Manager – 35. Gianluca Vialli, Italy.

TWITTER YE NOT

'Shout out to my homeboy Didier Drogba and tha Chelsea squad 4 winning tha Champions League! 1st time Uhearme #execbranch.'
US rapper Snoop Dogg reacting to the Champions League final

IT'LL NEVER CATCH ON

In 1964, Chelsea's thrusting young manager Tommy Docherty, impressed by the all-white strip of Real Madrid, ditched Chelsea's traditional white shorts for an all-blue kit. Not everyone was happy. 'I feel sure that, upon a vote, the majority of Chelsea FC supporters would prefer the old colour scheme to the new all-blue strip,' wrote Peter Post of Southall in September. 'Certainly modernise the style, but why change the colours round? I have followed Chelsea since I was five, signed on amateur forms for you through Mr Stewart Davidson in 1947, and am reluctant to see this change become a permanent one.' Post's letter was in vain: the Blues never returned to white shorts.

COIFFEUR, COPPER, DRAWER, CLERK

Full-back George Barber, who played the whole of the 1930s for Chelsea, was renowned throughout football as 'The only man who can stop Stanley Matthews.' Off the field, though, he was a man of many parts. Before football he had been a railway clerk, and took lessons in draughtsmanship which made him a keen cartoonist. Having married a hairdresser, he took up the profession himself and ran salons in Barking. And in the run-up to war he had joined the Met's Police War Reserve, becoming a fully-fledged East End copper in 1939.

IT'LL NEVER CATCH ON

'Read what J.G. COCK – The Famous Centre Forward – says of FINGA FOOTA: "Dear Sir, I think it is the best game I have seen. It is the nearest approach to the real game of football in the field. I quite amused myself and my friends for the evening (signed) J.G. Cock, Chelsea Centre Forward."'

Some way in fact from being akin to the 'real game' (even in 1920), 'Finga Foota' consisted of cardboard cutouts of footballers that fitted over a down-turned hand, the first two fingers intended to act as legs, and 'kick' the ball into a goal.

SPECIAL ONE

'Our group is a special group. Nobody can say we don't deserve this because we did it absolutely magnificently.'

José Mourinho, on the evening his team secured the Premier League title in 2005

ENGLISH CLUBS' EUROPEAN TROPHIES

Liverpool	8
Manchester United	4
Chelsea	3
Tottenham	3

THEY ALSO SERVE

Wally Lumsden, matchday steward, 1960s – 1980s.

'It was, "Are you good and loyal?", "who recommended you?", and that was good enough. The chief steward's place was a workman's shed near the old ivy-covered offices. On a match day we would congregate there and each man was sent to his post, mine being the old North Stand. The steward numbers stayed pretty static over the years, just covering new stands when they opened. There were around four of us to a block and that was quite ample to handle the crowd most of the time.

'Mind you, I did see some bad incidents down there. Once when Nottingham Forest visited, they all massed up causing trouble and I saw a very young lad get hit and his head split open. That was upsetting.

'But in general the people in the North Stand were nice. You had the celebrities of course. I was up there the famous day Raquel Welch came up there. The chairman allowed her to have brandy in the stand because she was so nervous – that's the story that came out, anyway – and I think she was half-cut by the time she left, walking along the side of the pitch shouting out to Ossie (God rest his soul).

'I used to pass [Lord] Attenborough and always touched my hat to him and his wife. There were quite a few characters, celebrities such as [comedy actor] Harry Fowler and [actor] Sam Kydd, and a lad from *Bless This House*, who went regularly then in my area. They were all fine, just blended in and wanted to watch Chelsea. Except [comedy actor] Jimmy Jewell, who was a bit "look at me", always laughing out loud with his big false teeth. It just added to the character of the place though.'

WINLESS STREAKS

Chelsea's longest league winless sequences are as follows:

12	home	6 Nov 1994 – 12 Apr 1995
22	away	4 Apr 1914 – 28 Apr 1915
21	both	2 Nov 1987 – 2 Apr 1988

In any competition, Chelsea's longest winless sequences are as follows:

11	home	19 Mar 1986 – 4 Oct 1986
26	away	11 Dec 1992 – 27 Dec 1993
15	both	3 Feb 1951 – 18 Apr 1951

THE ROAD TO MUNICH (3)

Buoyed by a sensational comeback against Napoli that confounded critics, Roberto Di Matteo's Chelsea faced Benfica in the quarter-finals with confidence, already knowing that Barcelona lay in wait as possible last-four opponents. There was less drama about the outcome of this two-legged affair largely because Ivorian forward

Salomon Kalou, with one of his priceless Champions League interventions, snatched a 1–0 win in the Estádio da Luz – the club's first away win of the campaign. He was set up astutely by Fernando Torres, the first of several timely contributions on the route to glory.

Needing the away goal but anxious not to concede, in the second leg the Portuguese attacked Chelsea, who were happy to stay solid and counter attack. The policy paid off when Ashley Cole was fouled in the area and Frank Lampard converted from the spot, and soon after Pereira marched off after seeing a second yellow card. The hosts enjoyed the best of several chances created, but then the ten men equalised from a corner, and the tension in the stadium was almost tangible. It was broken exquisitely, Mikel capping a superb performance by simultaneously clearing danger and setting Raul Meireles free. The former Porto midfielder covered the yards and shot high into the net, provoking a huge reaction of relief and joy. And so to Barcelona again . . .

NO LAUGHING MATTER

Three seasons before his elevation to legend status as skipper of Chelsea's 1954/55 league title winners, centre forward Roy Bentley was briefly responsible for striking of a different sort. He and team-mate Johnny Harris refused to sign up for the 1951/52 season – the team was so poor and they were not earning enough. 'My team must have been the biggest joke in football,' Roy later wrote, 'but I wasn't paid a comedian's salary.' The indignant pair stood firm for eight weeks without their salary – £12 per week after tax. 'Johnny and I spent the preseason training period playing golf,' Roy explained, 'although we talked football all the time . . . we walked along the Thames embankment, near to tears over Chelsea.'

French and Colombian teams offered Bentley a way out, then Chelsea directors caved in and dealt with the two players' grievances. Bentley returned to action on 8 September 1951, scoring in six of his first seven matches.

LEARNING TO BEAT BARÇA

'One of the reasons why we didn't play well [at Barcelona in 2005] was a little team tactical mistake. So for the second game I want to make a change. For the first time, instead of playing with Makelele and the "open triangle", we played Makelele and Lampard [together], and Gudjohnsen in behind. And it was February, so we had eight months of routine and I want to change. And I push the players to tell me that.

'They couldn't tell me objectively. They felt something. And they were saying to me, "It was difficult to press Xavi."

'"Why?"

'"Because my distance to Xavi was too big. So I want to press him, but when I arrive there the ball is not there. So I had to go there and I had to come back. I felt much more tired, because I had to go and when I go there, the ball is not there. So maybe it's better instead of playing with the open triangle, we play with Eidur in that position and Eidur is already on Xavi. So when we lose the ball, he's already there."

'"Yes that's for sure, if he's there he doesn't need to run 20 metres to go there, he's there. We have to change our shape, we have to think different, but to solve this problem, it's easy to solve the problem with that change."

'So we spoke one day, we spoke two days, on the third day I was saying to them my decision is this one.'

Chelsea won that Champions League second round second leg fixture against Barcelona 4–2 at Stamford Bridge, clinching the tie 5–4 on aggregate

GOALSCORING KEEPERS

Goalies who outwitted their counterpart on the opposing team.

Ben Baker, Chelsea 1–0 Bradford City, 19 November 1921, Division One – an 87th-minute penalty, and only goal of the game. (Baker also had one saved at Highbury in January 1922.)

Peter Bonetti, Chelsea 5–1 Charlton, 21 April 1969, Bobby Tambling's Testimonial – took and scored two penalties in the 27th and 61st minutes.

Dave Beasant Chelsea 5–1 Tottenham Hotspur, 27 March 1995, Kerry Dixon's Testimonial – hit the net while playing as an outfield player.

WHEN JOSÉ LOST IT

'We were losing 2–1 at half time [at Arsenal] and [José] wasn't happy. He gave them a rollicking along the lines of: "The best team is losing 2–1. We've been the best team, we've been better than Arsenal, we're doing this, we're doing that, but we're losing 2–1. How can this be possible? You come to places like this, you have to impose yourselves on the game."

'He was working himself up into a little bit of a frenzy. He picked up a plastic cup and assumed it was empty but it had a little bit of Lucozade at the bottom. So the players are all that way, and the staff are standing behind him – and he dropped it and volleyed it back towards the staff thinking it's empty. But there was a little bit of Lucozade that came flying out right into my face. Carlo Cudicini was next to me and it's gone all over Carlo's clothes.

'And he's ranting and raving and then he's picked up a tub of Vaseline and he's heaved that as well, and it's bounced off the wall in the dressing room and there's a big blob of Vaseline stuck on the wall, but slowly falling down towards the fitness coach's clothes.

'And I'm thinking, "What can I do? I can't tell the manager to fuck off." He'd just drowned me in Lucozade, it was running down my face.

'No one really noticed because the players were focused on the manager, but all the staff were looking at this Vaseline dripping down the wall. And the fitness coach is going to try to cover his clothes and I'm trying to grab a towel.

'He was in the middle of his talk so on one wanted to interrupt him, because it was crucial. So I'm trying to grab a towel to wipe the Lucozade off my face, and Carlo's trying to wipe the stuff off his gear, and the fitness coach is trying to make sure the Vaseline doesn't fall on his clothes.

'And at the time it wasn't funny because you're so focused on the game. We're all as intense as the manager, and we're thinking, "Get them ready for the second half".

But when you look back on it now, it was funny. It worked. But the boss didn't realise what he'd done. After the game he said: "I'm sorry, I'm sorry."'

Assistant manager Steve Clarke, 2005

LETTERS OF NOTE

'From now on we wish the Fulham Road end to be called "The Shed". This is the section where the fanatics stand – and while we are on fanatics, why don't more people some in the Shed and join in the singing and chanting, not just at big games like last season's Fairs Cup?'

Supporter Clifford Webb, Leicester City matchday programme, September 1966

HOME FIRES BURNING

In 2009, between the draws with Barcelona and APOEL in the Champions League, Chelsea established a new club record for consecutive home wins in all competitions of 12 (the previous best was 11 set in 2005/06.)

Chelsea 2–0 Blackburn Rovers, 17 May (Premier League)
Chelsea 2–1 Hull City, 15 Aug (Premier League)
Chelsea 3–0 Burnley, 29 Aug (Premier League)
Chelsea 1–0 Porto, 15 Sep (Champions League)
Chelsea 3–0 Tottenham Hotspur, 20 Sep (Premier League)
Chelsea 1–0 QPR, 23 Sep (League Cup)
Chelsea 2–0 Liverpool, 4 Oct (Premier League)
Chelsea 4–0 Atlético Madrid, 21 Oct (Champions League)
Chelsea 5–0 Blackburn Rovers, 24 Oct (Premier League)
Chelsea 4–0 Bolton Wanderers, 28 Oct (League Cup)
Chelsea 1–0 Manchester United, 8 Nov (Premier League)
Chelsea 4–0 Wolverhampton Wanderers, 21 Nov (Premier League)

GAME OF THE DECADE: THE 2010s

Chelsea 1–1 Bayern Munich, Champions League final, 15 May 2012
From 1905 to 19.05 . . . the greatest night in Chelsea's history
was delivered courtesy of Didier Drogba's equaliser, Petr Cech's
saves, and Drogba's iconic winning spot-kick. Extraordinary,
unforgettable, and on the Germans' home soil.

LETTERS OF NOTE

'I have found more vocal support away from home because there
is not the atmosphere at the Bridge for shouting for the Blues. If
everyone capable of cheering would shout powerfully at every
home game (especially early on in the game), then Chelsea will
know they have supporters on the terraces and Chelsea would be
inspired by such support.'

**Supporter Mick Greenaway, Workington Town matchday
programme, December 1964**

DOUBLE FIGURES OF FUN

Managers who have lost ten or more times to Chelsea, in
percentage order.

Mark Hughes	2004–12	13 defeats (76% of matches)
Steve Bruce	1999–2011	13 (65%)
Steve Coppell	1988–2008	13 (62%)
Sam Allardyce	2001–10	11 (61%)
Alan Curbishley	1998–2008	11 (61%)
Johnny Harris	1961–73	11 (61%)
Harry Redknapp	1988–2012	20 (56%)
Wilf Gillow	1926–39	11 (55%)
David Moyes	2002–12	17 (55%)
Martin O'Neill	1996–2012	12 (55%)
Bobby Robson	1969–2004	16 (55%)
Frank Hill	1948–63	10 (53%)
Rafael Benítez	2004–10	12 (46%)

Jim Smith	1975–2001	12 (46%)
Bob Kyle	1907–24	10 (45%)
Bill Murray	1946–57	10 (45%)
Matt Gillies	1959–72	12 (41%)
John Nicholson	1907–31	11 (41%)
Charles Foweraker	1920–39	10 (40%)
Joe Mercer	1955–74	12 (40%)
Frank Buckley	1924–55	12 (39%)
Howard Wilkinson	1982–2002	11 (39%)
Alan Brown	1954–70	12 (38%)
Bill Nicholson	1960–74	13 (38%)
Harry Potts	1958–79	11 (38%)
Tony Waddington	1962–75	12 (38%)
Vic Buckingham	1953–67	10 (36%)
Brian Clough	1968–93	12 (32%)
Fred Everiss	1905–38	14 (31%)
Arsène Wenger	1997–2012	13 (30%)
Alex Ferguson	1987–2012	19 (28%)
Matt Busby	1946–71	12 (26%)

Mark Hughes and Johnny Harris both won trophies while playing for Chelsea. Joe Mercer and Matt Busby were wartime guest players.

SCOUTING FOR BLUES

In between his coaching stints at Fulham and Ipswich (November 1968 to January 1969) Bobby Robson was put on the Chelsea payroll by manager Dave Sexton as an opposition scout. While observing Town's tactics at a game shortly before the Blues' Boxing Day encounter with them, he was approached by an Ipswich director and was in the Portman Road driving seat a few days later. He would stay with the Tractor Boys for 13 seasons, winning the FA Cup and UEFA Cup, and his contribution is commemorated in a statue outside Portman Road.

LETTERS OF NOTE

'During Chelsea's first season the player-manager, John Tait Robertson, made a chance discovery destined to have immense influence on the club's fortunes. Going to a Fulham v West Ham Reserves match to watch one of the latter's half-backs who had been recommended to him, Robertson was at once struck by the form of a nineteen-year-old inside-left playing for the same team, declaring the lad should make an ideal centre forward, and resolving to obtain him if possible at the end of the season.

'This he did, no transfer fee being involved. Player's name was George Hilsdon. Put straight into Chelsea's League eleven, at centre forward, for the opening match of the season, Hilsdon scored five goals which must surely be a record for any player making his League debut. Within a month he had been given his first cap – to score a hat-trick against Ireland in the Inter-League game at Belfast. Five other caps in full international matches followed in quick succession. (I still recall Jackie's excited whisper as he said: "Never heed yon half, juist watch that young inside-left; whit's his name? Hilleston, ye say? I must get him for us next season; he'll make a champion centre forward, ye marrk my words.")'

'Godfather' of Chelsea FC, Frederick Parker, recalling
the early days, 31 January 1939

MATCHDAY MEMORIES

'The image I've got, Boxing Day all the men and the boys would go over to the match and you could come back for your Christmas dinner. You'd all go over there on the bus, or sometimes in a car, and people would be wearing their new yellow gloves that they used to get. It was one of the traditional Christmas presents: new yellow gloves, and Will's Whiffs.

'Everyone was feeling very expansive. And sometimes of course you'd take whiskey with you, not for the kids, and they would pass the whiskey round and smoke the Will's Whiffs and everyone felt really really affluent. And you know it was a great feeling, a great feeling.'

The late Lord Stratford, Tony Banks, in 2005

THE ROAD TO MUNICH (4)

The sting in the tail of beating Benfica was that the 'best team in the world', led by the world's greatest footballer, stood between Chelsea and the bierkellers of Munich. More troubling, the second leg would be at Camp Nou – where the Blues have rarely fared well. The opening encounter at the Bridge was an extraordinary tactical affair, Chelsea ceding possession to the multi-passing Catalans, forcing them to use the wings more than they like. To cap a resolute first half, in which Sanchez's clip onto the bar was the closest Barça came to a breakthrough, the Blues took the lead in stoppage time, Ramires on the break cutting the ball square and Didier Drogba driving past Valdes. The Catalans found no recourse through the Londoners' rearguard and limped back to Spain screaming about 'anti-football' and 'injustice'. Few expected Roberto Di Matteo's men to hold out a second time, at Camp Nou, and when the Blues were 2–0 down with John Terry sent off, it took a form of madness to foresee the outcome. The game changed just before the break again when Frank Lampard produced the through-ball of the season for Ramires – playing right-back after an injury to Gary Cahill – to chip in the goal of the season. Suddenly the ten men were heading for the Allianz Arena. Dumbfounded, Barcelona rallied fiercely but with increasingly predictable impotence. Messi, world football's poster boy, even missed a penalty. Drogba, filling in as an auxiliary left-back, was replaced late on by Fernando Torres, and in time added on the Spaniard banished his well-publicised troubles with a stunning breakaway goal from Ashley Cole's desperate long clearance. This unforgettable tie finished 2–2, and Chelsea had reached the final for the second time in five seasons.

FRONTLINE FOOTBALLS

In early December 1914 the *Chelsea FC Chronicle* explained the presence of charity collectors at the Sheffield Wednesday match. 'The whole of today's collection will be devoted to the purchase of footballs for our gallant Tommies,' the programme said. 'Already we have 50 applications from various regiments, so when the boxes come round, do your bit for the boys who are doing their bit for you!'

In late December 1914 a list of recipients of those 50 footballs was published, and it is distinctly possible some the 'Chelsea balls' were among those said to have been used in matches with German troops during the famous truce of Christmas Day and Boxing Day that year.

Grateful troops sent letters to the *Chronicle*. 'Many thanks for ball,' wrote Private C.S. Dewar, 5th Royal Berkshire. 'Not even six inches of mud will stop us from using it.' Sgt C.A. Watts was equally delighted: 'On behalf of the NCOs & men of F Company, 25th City of London (the majority of whom are from Chelsea and neighbourhood) I thank you for the football. Whenever we use it we will think of the "Boys in Blue" who so kindly provided it.'

STIFF AS A BOARD

In the mid-1930s Chelsea's boardroom was devastated by the unexpected loss of four hugely experienced figures in swift succession. Firstly assistant club secretary Albert Palmer, a fixture of the Bridge hierarchy since 1907, died on 21 August 1935, aged 57. Little over a month later, on 27 September 1935, founding director Joseph Theophilus Mears (brother of the club's late owner, Gus) passed away. Joe's death at 64 years of age especially increased the off-field uncertainty because he had been acting as chairman while the incumbent, Claude Kirby, fought a long-standing illness. Mears was immediately succeeded by Charles 'Bill' Pratt Senior, and 67-year-old Kirby, chairman from the very first days in 1905, soon succumbed on 24 October 1935. Extraordinarily, Pratt himself was in place for just four months before dying on 19 February 1936 at the age of 70. Some stability was restored when Charles Pratt (son of the recently deceased) was made a director and Colonel C.J. Crisp, on the board for a decade, was put in the chair. Joe Mears Jr, a director since 1931, succeeded Crisp in 1940 until his death in 1966; Charles Pratt Jr died two years later.

BUTTER FINGERS

A supporter from Clapham was at Chelsea v Manchester City on Boxing Day 1914, and ducked when a terrace sweets vendor wildly threw a packet of nougat towards a buyer. The result was that the nougat struck the man behind in the face and cut him. Imagine the supporter's surprise when he recognised the victim as famous Surrey and England cricketer Jack Hobbs.

WHAT FOOTBALLERS DID AFTER FOOTBALL

'They weren't the best businessmen. They'd have everyone in for Sunday lunch and drink so much they'd forget to ask people for any money.'

**Fred Ward, who took over the Union Inn, Old Windsor,
from previous landlords and former Chelsea stars,
Ian Hutchinson and Peter Osgood**

IN WHICH WE SERVE

'Whereabouts of Players who were on the club's books at the beginning of the season may be of interest: The following joined the Police War Reserve: Alexander, Barber, Buchanan, Burgess, Foss, Griffiths, Hanson, Jackson, Mills, O'Hare, Payne, Salmond, Sherborne, Smale, Smith A.J., Spence, Tennant, Vaux, Weaver and Woodley. Bidewell and Mayes are serving in His Majesty's Fighting Forces, and of the remainder: Argue, White, Kilpatrick, McMillan and Creighton have returned to Scotland, Mitchell has joined his family in Ireland, James is at home in Wales and Smith, our recruit from Wales, has returned to the Midlands and will assist his former club until he attains military age and receives the call to the Colours.'

Chelsea FC Chronicle, **30 September 1939**

LOVE CONQUERS ALL

'Why have you avoided us, eluded us, for so long? Why have you punished us so much? For all these years you have flirted with us, tempted us, then run away.

'We thought you would come to us at Anfield twice, but you did not listen. Then in Moscow, you made us believe you were ours but turned your back, refused to let us touch you. Against Barcelona, again, you tortured us, made us want you even more, made it even harder.

'And even tonight, you hurt us first. Made us suffer. Made us fear it would be the same again, the late goal, the penalty kick, until the end. And now, at last, you belong to us.'

Match-winner Didier Drogba, flirting with the Champions League trophy during his impromptu speech in the dressing room after Chelsea's victory

STAMFORD BLITZ

The roof of the newly opened North Stand at Stamford Bridge was damaged in a raid by the Luftwaffe in 1945. The damage was swiftly repaired and supporters were soon back paying 3s a seat to watch matches in comfort.

DON'T PANIC

Stamford Bridge remained open for business throughout the Second World War, though obviously finances were tighter. The club relied on paying customers and when a midweek German air raid left an unexploded bomb on the terraces, manager Billy Birrell acted immediately. He rang civil defence to request the presence of a bomb disposal expert but was told there were none available for a few days. 'But we have a match on Saturday!' Birrell protested, to no avail.

And so, minutes later, he could be seen perched in his tweeds on the stadium terrace, smoking his pipe, and defusing the incendiary device by himself. The bomb rendered harmless, the match went ahead.

LETTERS OF NOTE

'I very much regret to have to inform you that your husband, No. F-74 Private R. Whiting, of this Battalion, was killed in action on the 28th of last month. He was killed instantaneously by shellfire in the recent offensive operations. Will you please accept my sincere sympathy in your loss. Your husband lost his life while attending to the wounded under fire, and died while doing his duty both well and nobly. He is buried very near the scene of the action near Vimy Ridge.'

Dated 15 May 1917 and sent to the widow of former Chelsea goalkeeper Bob Whiting by 2nd Lieutenant J.G. Howard, of the 17th Middlesex – the 'Footballers' Battalion'

BOX-TO-BOX

Post-Second World War winger Billy Gray, who died in 2011, supplemented his income by visiting schools in Battersea to teach the principles of boxing.

CAT 3

Peter Bonetti – 'The Cat' – is the third highest-ranked England goalkeeper based on fewest goals conceded per game, with an average of 0.57 over his seven appearances. Ahead of him are Joe Corrigan (0.56 per game) and Paul Robinson (0.54).

EVERYONE KNOWS YOU'RE BALD

In the 1930s a follicly-challenged Chelsea player from Ireland, Tom Priestley, wore a rugby-style skullcap on the pitch and a wig off it. No one was fooled.

THE ROAD TO MUNICH (5)

Chelsea's second Champions League final would be played the hard way – at the home ground of opponents, Bayern Munich. For sponsorship reasons the Allianz Arena was referred to as the 'Football Arena, Munich', but any neutrality was an illusion, especially when the Bayern end unfurled banners saying 'Our City, Our Stadium, Our Cup.' Worse, the Blues had to reorganise without the suspended Ramires, Branislav Ivanovic, Raul Meireles and John Terry, all of whom had played an important part in the campaign to date. In the event, it transpired Bayern's loss of defensive screens Luiz Gustavo, David Alaba and Holger Badstüber was the more costly. In contrast Chelsea's rearguard was once more the outstanding unit on the pitch, brilliantly assisted by Mikel and Frank Lampard in midfield and, in a successful gamble, young Ryan Bertrand on the left of midfield. The German hosts carried the swagger of their fans in the city's bierkellers into the live arena, with former Blue Arjen Robben buzzing, but the depleted visitors restricted Bayern to snatched attempts until the 82nd minute, when Thomas Muller's downward header eluded the otherwise faultless Petr Cech. Chelsea's chances of a response in time remaining relied more than ever on one-man army Didier Drogba. He did not let his club down. When Torres won a corner down the right, Juan Mata curled the ball in short and the Ivorian shrugged off Jerome Boateng, rose high and muscled his header past Manuel Neuer to equalise. Momentum swung the Blues' way in the initial period of extra time, before Drogba caught Franck Ribéry's heel and Robben stepped up to the spot. Mikel, his old team-mate, psyched him out by reminding him how good Cech was, and the Dutchman's poor penalty was duly saved.

No one present at the Moscow final in 2008 needed reminding of the outcome of that penalty shoot-out. Mata, Chelsea's player of the season, missed the first. Bayern were note perfect until their fourth, Chelsea's Luiz and Lampard keeping pace to make it 2–3. Cech, who had guessed right every time, saved substitute Ivica Olic's effort, though, and the Germans' hands slipped off the trophy. Ashley Cole converted to level the scores. Now Bastian Schweinsteiger – surprisingly sat down in his own penalty area, unable to watch when Robben took his extra-time penalty –

walked towards the spot. He looked anxious and rightly so, because Cech read him and tipped his shot onto the post. The Chelsea supporters were suddenly abuzz with the realisation that the next kick could win the European Cup. It was Drogba who broke from the group to stroll forward, adjusting his clothing, his laces, his shin pads, gathering his thoughts. Then a run-up – too short, screamed some – and Neuer was sent the wrong way, the ball softly nestling in the net. The Ivorian reeled away in tears of joy and celebrated in front of the Blues faithful. The Champions League, that holy grail of the Abramovich era, had been claimed at last.

Chelsea (4-2-3-1): Cech; Bosingwa, Cahill, David Luiz, Cole; Mikel, Lampard (C); Kalou (Torres 83), Mata, Bertrand (Malouda 73); Drogba

Unused subs: Turnbull, Ferreira, Essien, Romeu, Sturridge

Scorer: Drogba 87

Booked: Cole 80, David Luiz 85, Drogba 93, Torres 119

Shoot-out penalties: Mata (missed), Luiz, Lampard, Cole, Drogba

Bayern Munich (4-2-3-1): Neuer; Lahm (c), Tymoshchuk, Boateng, Contento; Schweinsteiger, Kroos; Robben, T. Muller (Van Buyten 85), Ribery (Olic 96); Gomez

Unused subs: Butt, Rafinha, Usami, Pranjic, Petersen

Scorer: Muller 82

Booked: Schweinsteiger 3

Shoot-out penalties: Lahm, Gomez, Neuer, Olic (missed), Schweinsteiger (missed)

Referee: Pedro Proença (Portugal)

Attendance: 62,500

STAT'S YOUR LOT

Chelsea scored 27 goals from group stage to final in winning the 2012 Champions League trophy. Only Real and Barça have ever won the competition scoring more goals over a campaign.

THE MEN WHO WOULD BE KINGS

'I think I could identify [the leaders at Chelsea] because of their style of play. When you are outside and you see players on the pitch, you can more or less smell it. I think what I did well with Lampard and Terry was to give them more power than they normally have in a dressing room. I give them the crown, you know?'

José Mourinho, 2005

MR CONSISTENCY

John Terry was named in the FIFA/FIFPro World Team of the Year for five consecutive seasons in 2005, 2006, 2007, 2008 and 2009 – the only player to achieve that feat. He has also made the most appearances as captain in Chelsea's history.

SPIRIT OF THE BLITZ

'Last weekend we had some enjoyable matches to watch when a number of grounds staged matches for the London Juniors. The air raid sirens sounded in the middle of the afternoon when play was in full swing, but no one worried. The youngsters were not in the smallest degree perturbed – nor were the thousands of people watching from the stands. At Stamford Bridge Mr Birrell, the Chelsea manager, stopped the game for a few minutes and told the boys they might leave the field if they wished. But the game went on, and only about a score of people left the stands. Even these few may easily have been wardens who had to go on duty when the alarm was given.'

Townsville Daily Bulletin, 31 October 1940

SMALL-SIDED GAME

We tend to think five-a-side football is a modern innovation. However, one of the many intriguing items on display at the Chelsea Museum is a trophy from the five-a-side tournament held during Romford's Charter Celebrations on 16 September 1937, won by Chelsea at Brooklands, Romford, Essex.

LETTERS OF NOTE

'Having followed Chelsea for ten years I wish to object most strongly to the manner in which I was referred to in the "Court Report" (Chelsea Programme, March 16th). I find the premise that one unfortunate incident is sufficient to nullify years of loyal support and good behaviour incredible.

'Yet this is what is implied by the use of inverted commas around the word "supporter". Taking it further, the conclusion is that I embarked on a lengthy journey, not to support Chelsea, but with the intention of committing a felony.

'The incident in question concerned my involvement in a mêlée after the Cup-tie with Sheffield Wednesday with followers of the home team, during which I was provoked into retaliation which subsequently proved both foolish and costly.

'A reasonable appraisal of the matter would not permit justification for the veiled sarcasm evident in your account of the affair. "To err is human – to forgive divine".'

Written by Hogan Burke to the Chelsea programme, April 1968

EUROPEAN FOOTBALL

By winning the Champions League in 2011/12, Chelsea scooped a record £49.2 million in TV broadcast rights and UEFA prize money. Manchester United were the next highest beneficiaries with £30.3m, followed by neighbours City (£23.4m), Arsenal (£23.1m), Stoke City (£4.2m), and Tottenham, Birmingham and Fulham (all £3.7m). Chelsea's greater slice of the TV pool cash resulted from the other Champions League sides crashing out early and therefore playing far fewer matches.

ROYAL PATRONAGE

When King George V paid a high-profile visit to Stamford Bridge for the FA Cup clash with Leicester on 21 February 1920, he arrived by motorcar and was greeted by the man who owned much of west London, Chelsea's club president, the Earl Cadogan.

Chairman Claude Kirby then took over, escorting His Majesty inside the ground where the band of the Irish Guards played the national anthem. He was afterwards presented to the players and watched the game from the comfort of the East Stand seats, apparently exchanging tactical observations with Kirby.

The only break with protocol was when a nearby supporter attempted to entice the king into buying a raffle ticket on the outcome of the match. This was a relief to the nervy monarch, who feared Communism was on the march and a show might be made, including the crowd singing 'The Red Flag'. Soon after the match he reported: 'I went to a football match at which there were 73,000; at the end everyone sang the National Anthem and cheered tremendously. There were no Bolsheviks there! At least I never saw any. The country is all right; just a few extremists are doing all the harm.'

This was far from the being the king's first visit to the Bridge. He had even attended a baseball match there on 26 February 1914. As if to reveal his affection for the stadium, for several years during his reign Windsor Castle and Stamford Bridge were linked by a marathon event, which started at the king's residence and ended with a lap at Chelsea's.

His patronage of the Pensioners in 1921 attracted national press coverage. Manchester-based *Athletic News* joked: 'If these kingly favours be continued the Chelsea club will soon be entitled to alter the sign over their gateway, and in golden letters blaze forth: "Royal Chelsea, Purveyor of Football to their Majesties King George of England and King Alphonso of Spain".'

Alfonso XIII, ruler of Spain, had previously been to Stamford Bridge as, reportedly, had the Sultan of Morocco.

OVER LAND AND SEA (AND LEICESTER)

Chelsea FC tours 1946–2012

1946 – Denmark, Switzerland

28 April	KB	Copenhagen	2–1 loss
30 April	Odense	Odense	3–0 win
26 May	Young Fellows Zurich	Zurich	5–0 win
30 May	Servette	Geneva	2–0 win
2 June	Young Boys	Bern	7–1 win
5 June	La Chaux-de-Fonds	La Chaux-de-Fonds	4–0 win
8 June	St Gallen	St Gallen	5–1 win

1947 – Sweden

3 June	IFK Norrköping	Norrköping	4–1 loss
8 June	Sweden XI	Stockholm	1–0 loss
11 June	Gothenburg XI	Gothenburg	0–0 draw

1949 – Malta

14 May	UK Services Malta	Valletta	6–0 win
15 May	Malta FA Select	Valletta	3–2 win
18 May	Hamrun/Sliema Select	Valletta	6–2 win

1950 – France, Italy

14 May	Lille Olympique	Lille	3–1 loss
8 June	Internazionale	Milan	1–0 loss
11 June	Sampdoria	Genoa	2–1 loss

1951 – Algeria

19 May	Algiers Combination	Algiers	2–1 win
21 May	Vienna	Algiers	4–0 win
26 May	Oran Combination	Oran	0–0 draw
27 May	Valladolid	Oran	2–1 win

1954 – Switzerland

30 Jan	Young Boys	Bern	3–0 loss
31 Jan	Servette	Geneva	1–0 loss

1954 – USA, Canada

9 May	Fortuna Dusseldorf	New York	3–2 win
16 May	Rangers	Montreal	1–0 loss
21 May	Baltimore Rockets	Baltimore	7–1 win
23 May	Borussia Dortmund	New York	6–1 loss
26 May	Eastern Seaboard All-Stars	Massachusetts	6–0 win
30 May	American All-Stars	New Jersey	2–0 win
5 June	Rangers	Toronto	4–1 win
6 June	Rangers	New York	0–0 draw

1955 – Ireland, France, Netherlands

2 May	Shamrock Rovers	Dublin	3–2 loss
7 May	Lens	Lens	1–1 draw
11 May	Holland XI	Amsterdam	2–2 draw
14 May	Rouen	Rouen	4–2 win

1957 – Netherlands

15 May	Feyenoord	Rotterdam	4–1 win
16 May	Fortuna 54	Geleen	2–2 draw

1958 – Bulgaria

10 August	CDNA	Sofia	2–1 loss
17 August	Levski	Sofia	2–0 win

1961 – Israel

1 May	Hapoel XI	Haifa	1–0 win
4 May	Israel XI	Tel Aviv	2–0 win
6 May	Maccabi XI	Tel Aviv	5–2 win

1964 – Barbados, Trinidad, Jamaica, Haiti

21 May	Barbados	Bridgetown	7–0 win
23 May	Wolves	Bridgetown	3–1 loss
26 May	Trinidad	Port of Spain	5–0 win
27 May	Wolves	Port of Spain	3–2 win
29 May	Wolves	Kingston	4–2 loss
31 May	St James XI	Montego Bay	15–0 win
2 June	Wolves	Kingston	3–0 win
3 June	St Mary's XI	Montego Bay	12–1 win

4 June	Jamaica XI	Kingston	4–1 win
6 June	Wolves	Port-au-Prince	2–0 win
7 June	Haiti	Port-au-Prince	

(match abandoned with Chelsea losing 2–1)

1965 – Australia

8 May	New South Wales	Sydney	5–0 win
12 May	Australian Capital Territory	Canberra	7–0 win
15 May	Northern New South Wales	Newcastle	6–2 win
16 May	Victoria	Melbourne	1–0 win
19 May	Western Australia	Perth	6–1 win
22 May	South Australia	Adelaide	2–1 win
23 May	Australian Select XI	Sydney	2–2 draw
26 May	Tasmania	Hobart	12–0 win
30 May	Australian World Cup XI	Melbourne	1–1 draw
2 June	South Coast XI	Wollongong	1–0 win
6 June	Queensland	Brisbane	4–0 win

1966 – Germany, Switzerland, Scotland

29 July	Turn-UND Sportverei	Eltingen	10–1 win
3 Aug	Lugano	Lugano	3–2 win
6 Aug	Stuttgart	Stuttgart	2–0 loss
8 Aug	Dundee	Dundee	2–1 win
12 Aug	Hamburg	Hamburg	3–1 loss
14 Aug	Eintracht Frankfurt	Frankfurt	1–0 loss

1967 – USA, Canada, Bermuda

25 May	Dundee	Los Angeles	4–2 loss
27 May	British Columbia All-Stars	Vancouver	5–2 win
28 May	North West All-Stars	Seattle	5–0 win
30 May	O'Keefe's Club	Victoria	3–2 win
4 June	Dundee	Hertford	2–2 draw
7 June	Devonshire Colts	Bermuda	8–0 win
9 June	Pembroke Hamilton Club	Bermuda	2–0 win
10 June	Bermuda Olympic XI	Bermuda	4–2 win
11 June	Eintracht Braunschweig	Boston	3–1 loss
13 June	Rochester	Rochester	6–1 win

1968 – Germany, Ireland

3 Aug	Kaiserslautern	Kaiserslautern	1–0 loss
10 Aug	Waterford	Cork	5–2 win

1969 – Mozambique

29 May	Mozambique XI	Maputo	2–1 win
5 June	Mozambique XI	Maputo	9–3 win

1970 – Venezuela, Barbados

10 May	Vitória Setúbal	Caracas	2–0 loss
12 May	Santos	Caracas	4–1 loss
19 May	Barbados XI	Bridgetown	4–1 win
26 May	Barbados XI	Bridgetown	4–0 win

1970 – Netherlands

26 July	Ajax	Amsterdam	1–1 draw
29 July	NAC Breda	Breda	3–2 loss
1 Aug	PSV	Eindhoven	2–0 loss

1971 – El Salvador, Trinidad

30 May	Southampton	San Salvador	8–3 win
1 June	El Salvador	San Salvador	1–0 win
4 June	Trinidad	Port of Spain	3–2 win
6 June	Southampton	Port of Spain	6–2 win

1971 – Sweden, Belgium

25 July	Halmstads	Halmstad	6–0 win
28 July	Stockholm XI	Stockholm	1–1 draw
1 Aug	Östers	Vaxjo	1–1 draw
4 Aug	Bruges	Bruges	1–1 draw

1972 – Barbados

18 May	Barbados Combined XI	Bridgetown	5–0 win
20 May	New South Wales	Bridgetown	4–1 win
23 May	Barbados Combined XI	Bridgetown	10–0 win

1973 – Iran

18 May	Persepolis	Tehran	1–1 draw
21 May	Taj Tehran	Tehran	1–0 win
25 May	Tehran XI	Tehran	1–0 loss

1974 – Australia

22 May	Northern Territories	Darwin	6–1 win
26 May	Western Australia	Perth	1–0 win
29 May	South Australia	Adelaide	4–0 win
2 June	Queensland	Brisbane	
	(match abandoned)		
7 June	Illawarra District	Wollongong	4–1 win
9 June	New South Wales	Sydney	2–1 loss

1977 – USA, Canada

25 May	Seattle Sounders	Seattle	2–0 loss
27 May	Vancouver Island All-Stars	Vancouver	3–0 win
1 June	San Jose Earthquakes	San José	2–1 win
3 June	Los Angeles Aztecs	Los Angeles	3–1 win

1977 – Sweden

26 July	Kalmar	Kalmar	1–1 draw
29 July	Malmö	Malmö	1–0 win

1978 – Norway

13 May	Jerv	Jerv	2–0 win
16 May	Voss	Voss	6–1 win
17 May	Hauger	Bærum	4–1 win

1978 – Spain, Portugal

9 Aug	Seville	Seville	3–2 loss
11 Aug	Porto	Porto	2–1 loss

1980 – Greece

10 Aug	Panathinaikos	Athens	2–0 loss
11 Aug	AEK	Athens	2–2 draw

1981 – Sweden

11 Aug	Västerås	Västerås	1–0 loss
12 Aug	Flens	Flen	2–0 win
14 Aug	BK Forward	Örebro	1–0 loss
17 Aug	Hofors	Hofors	2–1 loss

1982 – Sweden, Finland

27 July	Östersund	Östersund	1–0 loss
30 July	Ångermanland	Sollefteå	2–1 win
1 Aug	Strömsund	Strömsund	8–0 win
3 Aug	Mariehamn	Mariehamn	6–1 win

1989 – Sweden, Norway

25 July	Mjölby	Mjölby	3–0 win
27 July	Norrstrands IF	Karlstad	2–0 win
30 July	Fryksdalen	Ämtervik	9–0 win

1990 – Sweden, Finland, Denmark

24 July	Helsingborgs IF	Helsingborg	1–1 draw
26 July	Rydöbruks IF	Rydöbruk	7–3 win
28 July	Väst-Nyland	Karjaa	3–0 win
30 July	Borås	Borås	6–0 win
1 Aug	Hvidovre IF	Hvidovre	2–1 win

1991 – Ireland

20 July	Limerick City	Limerick	4–1 win
23 July	Bohemians	Dublin	2–0 win
26 July	Sligo Rovers	Sligo	4–0 win

1992 – Canada

15 May	Vancouver Island All-Stars	Victoria	2–1 win
18 May	Dundee United	Vancouver	3–0 win
20 May	Vancouver 89ers	Vancouver	2–2 draw

1992 – Ireland, Northern Ireland

19 July	Sligo Rovers	Sligo	2–2 draw
21 July	Derry City	Derry	1–1 draw
23 July	Portadown	Portadown	3–0 win
25 July	Cork City	Cork	2–1 win

1997 – Hong Kong, Brunei, Thailand

20 May	South China	Hong Kong	3–2 win
24 May	Brunei	Bandar Seri Begawan	6–0 win
27 May	Thailand	Bangkok	1–0 win

1998 – Martinique

| 15 May | Auxerre | Fort-de-France | 3–0 loss |
| 17 May | Martinique Club XI | Fort-de-France | 3–1 win |

2003 – Malaysia

25 July	Malaysia	Kuala Lumpur	4–1 win
27 July	Newcastle	Kuala Lumpur	0–0 draw
		(5–4 win on penalties)	

2004 – USA

24 July	Celtic	Seattle	4–2 win
29 July	Roma	Pittsburgh	3–0 win
2 August	AC Milan	Philadelphia	3–2 loss

2005 – USA

24 July	AC Milan	Foxborough	1–0 win
28 July	DC United	Washington DC	2–1 win
31 July	AC Milan	New Jersey	1–1 draw

2006 – USA

| 5 August | MLS All-Stars | Chicago | 1–0 loss |

2007 – USA

14 July	Club América	Stanford	2–1 win
17 July	Suwon Bluewings	Los Angeles	1–0 win
21 July	LA Galaxy	Los Angeles	1–0 win

2008 – China, Malaysia, Russia

23 July	Guangzhou Pharmaceutical	Guangzhou	4–0 win
26 July	Chengdu Blades	Macau	7–0 win
29 July	Malaysia Select XI	Kuala Lumpur	2–0 win
1 Aug	Lokomotiv Moscow	Moscow	1–1 draw
		(5–4 loss on pens)	
3 Aug	AC Milan	Moscow	5–0 win

2009 – USA

18 July	Seattle Sounders	Seattle	2–0 win
21 July	Internazionale	Pasadena	2–0 win
24 July	AC Milan	Baltimore	2–1 win
26 July	Club América	Dallas	2–0 win

2011 – Malaysia, Thailand, China

21 July	Malaysian XI	Kuala Lumpur	1–0 win
24 July	Thai All-Stars	Bangkok	4–0 win
27 July	Kitchee	Hong Kong	4–0 win
30 July	Aston Villa	Hong Kong	2–0 win

2012 – USA

19 July	Seattle Sounders	Seattle	4–2 win
23 July	Paris Saint-Germain	New York	1–1 draw
25 July	MLS All-Stars	Philadelphia	3–2 loss
28 July	AC Milan	Miami	1–0 loss

BLACKPOOL COWER

Chelsea players who left the field of play early in Arctic conditions at Bloomfield Road on 29 October 1932:

Willie Ferguson (cramp)
Peter O'Dowd (felt faint)
Len Allum (cold)
Harry Miller (cold)
Eric Oakton (cold)

EASY COME

'PS Winston Bogarde was signed with Luca's knowledge and approval.'

Managing director Colin Hutchinson's response to criticism of the acquisition of former Barcelona defender Bogarde, notoriously paid £10 million over four seasons while making just nine appearances. Despite those inflated wages, Bogarde was declared bankrupt in 2011

KIND OF BLUE

Former Zombies lead singer Colin Blunstone is the nephew of long-serving Blues winger Frank Blunstone.

BY JOSH

On 15 September 2010 against Žilina, Chelsea's Josh McEachran became the first Champions League participant to have been born after the competition changed format from the European Cup in 1992/3. He came on as a substitute and was aged 17 years, 198 days.

STILL THE GREATEST?

In January 2003 an official poll aimed to determine who supporters of the day regarded as Chelsea's all-time greatest players. This was the result:

1.   Gianfranco Zola
2.   Peter Osgood
3.   Dennis Wise
4.   Jimmy Greaves
5.   Kerry Dixon
6.   Ruud Gullit
7.   Peter Bonetti
8.   Charlie Cooke
9.   Gianluca Vialli
10. Jimmy Floyd Hasselbaink

The gifted Italian forward scooped 60 per cent of votes cast, a reward for the pleasure he had given fans over six years and nigh-on 300 appearances in the famous royal blue. A month later, when he passed that landmark Zola removed his shirt to reveal a vest with a thank you message for supporters: '300 wonderful times.' His former team-mate Mark Hughes once described him leaving opposition defenders 'with twisted blood', so bamboozling was his imagination.

The most successful period in the club's history was yet to unfold, though. How different would the results be now?

ACKNOWLEDGEMENTS

With thanks to Paul Dutton, Paul Mason, Robert Stein, Chelsea FC Communications team, Chelsea FC Museum, the Chelsea Twitterati, and all Blues supporters around the globe. My gratitude also to Michelle Tilling and The History Press team.